FABULOUS FRED

The Strife and Times of Fred Cook

Published by Melbourne Books
Level 9, 100 Collins Street,
Melbourne, VIC 3000
Australia
www.melbournebooks.com.au
info@melbournebooks.com.au

Title: Fabulous Fred: The Strife and Times of Fred Cook
Author: Paul Amy
ISBN: 9781922129475

A catalogue record for this book is available from the National Library of Australia

Front and back cover photos: Newspix / News Limited

FABULOUS FRED

The Strife and Times of Fred Cook

Paul Amy

Foreword by Sam Newman

M

MELBOURNE BOOKS

Paul Amy

Dedicated to my father, Bill Amy (1941–1995),
who is thought of every day.

Fred Cook

To my parents, Fred and Shirley Cook

Foreword

It is a challenge to dislike Fred Cook. A persuasive, laconic, rambling raconteur, he is a flawed gemstone.

In his heyday he captivated sporting crowds as an icon of the country's second-tier Australian Rules football competition of the day, the Victorian Football Association. There was no bigger name in the VFA than Fred Cook, or 'Fabulous Fred', as his legions of fans called him.

But he succumbed to the pressures of a pop-star, Hollywood lifestyle, and he paid dearly for the romance.

His foray into the hospitality industry as the proprietor of Port Melbourne's Station Hotel gave his extroverted life another kick, and his constant companions were the elite movers and shakers of society. As sure as night follows day, the opportunists, those detecting a chance to exploit, and the criminal underclass gradually permeated his person.

This is the classic chronological rise-and-fall story of sex, drugs and rock-and-roll, made all the meretricious by a large dose of sport — except this ain't no story!

Sam Newman
June 2014

1

IT had been an unremarkable day in the Frankston Magistrates' Court.

Locals, a few of them carrying the whiff of aftershave and looking uncomfortable in just-bought suits, had come to answer charges like drink-driving, burglary and theft. They filed in before 10am and they hoped their solicitors would ensure they filed out.

Quick-with-a-quip prosecutor Ricky Lewis would have called it a 'mixed bag' of cases, as he invariably did when quizzed by the reporter covering proceedings for the *Frankston Standard* newspaper.

Most cases were heard in court one, in a building that stood for years on Davey Street, only a couple of decent drop punts from the Frankston football ground. But around lunchtime on this day in December 1991, court staff began to murmur about a matter to be heard in the smaller second court.

A former footballer had been arrested, they said. Big name in his day, apparently.

A few minutes later, uniformed police marched a handcuffed and dishevelled Fred Cook in to court. Sweat beaded on his forehead. He wore jeans that needed a wash, a similarly grubby white shirt and running shoes on their last legs.

Some wouldn't have recognised him as the man who less than a decade earlier was the most captivating and colourful player in the Victorian Football Association (VFA). Supporters called the prolific Port Melbourne goalkicker 'Fabulous Fred'. He assumed the profile of a pop star.

Police had come to know him well, too, but as Frederick William Cook, repeat offender. To them he was no football hero. He was just another sloppy crook who needed locking up. 'Fred Cook? Can't stay out of trouble. He's a pain in the arse,' an officer from the Frankston District Support Group once replied when asked about the former Port champion.

A pin-up boy to an ocean of small fry, Cook kicked bags of goals in his sponsored Puma boots and was integral in six Port Melbourne premierships during the historic club's most successful era.

Its successor, the Victorian Football League (VFL), has struggled for publicity for years. But the VFA had a large and fanatical following in the 1970s and 1980s — it was common for fans to support a league team on Saturdays and an association team on Sundays — and a cluster of great players and compelling characters. There was Dandenong spearhead Jim 'Frosty' Miller. Feared Preston ruckman Harold Martin. Cook's Port Melbourne teammate and champion big man Vic 'Stretch' Aanensen. Bearded Coburg swashbuckler Phil Cleary. Rugged Sandringham defender Alf Beus. Geelong West sharpshooter Joe Radojevic. Long after retirement, their names still resonate with seasoned football followers.

But Cook had the largest profile of all. Wearing the No. 5 jumper from full forward, he was the finisher for a team as bruising as it was brilliant. With his regular starring roles in matches televised by Channel 0, he helped haul the VFA out of the shadows and into the spotlight.

The Encyclopedia of League Footballers, recording Cook's thirty-three games for Footscray between 1967 and 1969, described him as 'one of the greatest stars to have played in the VFA', formed in 1877. 'His goalkicking feats with Port were legendary,' it said.

Former Footscray champion Doug Hawkins said, 'He was the king of the VFA, Freddie, the absolute king.'

And he had charisma bursting from his boots. 'Although he appeared apologetic about the manner in which he humiliated opponents, the cameras were drawn to him,' Cleary wrote in his book *Cleary Independent*. 'At after-match gatherings, he wandered through the throng like a film star.'

Women loved him, and he them. He had a legion of ladies, including the daughter of a country's Prime Minister and a television soap star. His great mate Sam Newman's reputation as a ladies' man endures. But he says he had nothing on Cook.

With the popular Station Hotel in Port Melbourne (home to Melbourne's most glamorous strippers, all cherrypicked by Cook) and newspaper, radio and TV gigs, he had the wealth to go with the adulation. But the famous footballer with the larrikin streak who mixed with Melbourne's sporting and entertainment elite became infamous for his drug use, his association with some of Melbourne's most notorious criminals and his spells in prison. He went from hero to zero in three years.

Cook had a gun put to his head. He was badly bashed when his associates thought he'd turned police informer. Newman was there to save him, and calls it the scariest day of his life. Cook witnessed violent assaults. He himself struck women. He went to his mother's funeral drugged to the eyeballs. He would inject himself in school yards ahead of lectures to students about the perils of drugs and alcohol.

Sitting in jail in a period of sobriety, he reflected on how far he'd fallen and how much he'd hurt his family. It was Christmas and he was aching to see his kids. He thought about killing himself.

Cook can pinpoint the start of his slide. One night he was battling the flu ahead of a sportsman's night alongside the St Kilda Brownlow Medal champion Neil Roberts and English fast bowler John Snow.

Hardened Melbourne criminal Dennis Allen, who'd started hanging around the Station, whipped out a bag of white powder and a pen knife and tipped some amphetamines into his drink. Cook immediately felt a burst of energy, and was ready to fulfill his engagement.

Up until then he'd relied on strong coffee (sweetened by five sugars) and cigarettes to stay 'up'.

But, with his every day crowded with work commitments, he began to lean on speed, and eventually his life fell apart. He admitted the drugs were a way of replacing the adrenaline rush football brought him. Cook lost everything he owned, and resorted to drug pushing and petty crime to get by.

Where once he featured in the sports pages for his deeds on football grounds, he now filled headlines in the news section for his court appearances. 'Footy star on drug counts'. 'Drugs bring down footy great'. 'Cook on bond over drugs'. 'Drugs nearly killed me — Cook'. 'Footy hero Cook jailed'. They piled up like rubble around a wrecking ball. In May 1989, he went before the Victorian County Court for drug trafficking and deception.

His legal counsel, Bruce Walmsley, told Judge Hanlon that Cook had 'demonstrated himself to be a pathetic figure'.

The judge released him on a bond and suspended sentence, commenting: 'In the end I have come to the view that the pathetic mess you made of your life by the use of the drug in which you trafficked is clearly a sufficient example to the community.'

Flanked by his de facto wife, Sally Desmond, Cook stood outside the County Court and declared he was going clean.

He'd lost his business and the respect of his family and friends, he said.

'Have I learned a lesson? Is the Pope a Catholic?' he said to reporters.

'If anything, it's a lesson to young people. If it isn't a lesson, I don't know what is. I certainly will not be dabbling in any more drugs.'

He said the same in an extended interview in the *Sun* newspaper with his pal and television colleague Newman the following year. 'I can't help anyone else until I help myself, but the life I lead is now way behind me and will never happen again.'

But it did, again and again. His list of convictions would eventually extend to twelve pages.

Newman, and many others, pleaded with him to apply to his life the discipline he showed in his football career. Cook was unable to act on the advice. He had believed he could use drugs to his advantage, squeezing a few extra hours into his busy days, but they took a sinister hold on him. He kicked hundreds of goals, but he couldn't kick his drug habit.

In April 1990, he was sent to prison for twelve months after breaching the suspended sentence by swiping cement and timber. He was working as a handyman and needed the materials to finish a job and provide for Desmond and their two-year-old son. The man who once put $10,000 a week into his pocket as a publican was now scratching to pay for nappies and milk.

After serving his time at Morwell River Prison Farm, Cook again swore he would stay out of trouble.

But old drug habits die hard. A few months later police searched his home and found amphetamines and cannabis.

Then came his appearance at Frankston Magistrates' Court. Police had performed another raid and found more amphetamines and $10,000 worth of stolen goods, a booty they called an 'Aladdin's Cave'.

Hooking up with young crooks, Cook had been swapping drugs for stolen gear for a month, stockpiling it in a unit. He was running it like a small business, keeping a ledger of the comings and goings.

It led to another stretch in prison. By that stage there was nothing fabulous about Fred. The champion spearhead who a few years earlier was surrounded by famous faces and adoring supporters had only four hard walls for company.

2

FRED Cook is back in Frankston Magistrates' Court in late March, 2014. But, having shaken his drug addiction a few years earlier, he is in far better shape than during his appearance there in 1991. At age sixty-six, he is looking pretty well for a man who has subjected his body to years of abuse. He carries a few extra kilos around the stomach, but nothing a few strolls around the block wouldn't fix.

He thinks he will be walking soon enough. Cook is in court for driving while disqualified. Twelve months earlier he'd been given a four-month jail term, suspended for two years, for the same offence and his long-time lawyer, Bernie Balmer, is warning him that he is facing prison. Cook's list of prior convictions for road-related offences runs to five pages.

Before mention of his case, Cook sits on the steps outside the court. He sucks on a cigarette as he flicks through the *Herald Sun* newspaper, settling on a photograph on the Confidential page of Sam Newman hamming it up with *Footy Show* colleague Shane Crawford.

He is sitting in sunlight, perspiring. 'I've got a headache and I'm worried,' he is saying. 'I mean, Christ, there were times I should have done time and didn't. They could have locked me up and thrown away the key. But I shouldn't do it over this.'

His mobile phone rings. It is his son Jordan wanting to know how he is getting on.

'What do you mean "old man"? I'll give you old man! Yeah, good, good, good. Haven't gone in yet. Just sitting outside having a smoke. Bernie's already in there. Let's hope he can work his miracle, hey? Come on Bernie, work that miracle.'

A short time later a middle-aged woman approaches. 'What are you doing, you silly old bastard?' she asks, laughing. Cook explains the driving offence. The woman replies that her partner, answering a charge of making threats to kill, had been arrested with trafficking marijuana as soon as he arrived at court. The woman and Cook go back a long way. He knew her husband, who had died of a heroin overdose about twenty years earlier.

Just before 10am, Cook walks to the court entrance, places his phone, car keys, cigarettes and a large blue diary into a plastic container, and is scanned through security.

His case is to be heard in court two, where the spiky-haired, moustached Balmer is seated at the bench talking to another defence counsel and the police prosecutor.

Cook nods at Balmer, takes a seat in the back row and begins to read the newspaper again.

He immerses himself in it as a few cases are heard: an eighteen-year-old woman up on ninety-six theft charges, a middle-aged man trying to shake a fraud charge over an insurance claim for damage to his car, and a younger man charged with the sexual assault of his former partner.

'The matter of Frederick Williams to court two please,' the female clerk says finally. Frederick Williams is Frederick William Cook. Fifteen years earlier, seeking to overcome a bad credit rating, he had changed his name by deed poll. An hour later he was opening bank accounts and being offered credit cards.

Cook has been fretting about the hearing for weeks, fearing another spell in prison. The case had been adjourned a few times while Balmer sought a psychiatric assessment and a pre-sentencing report.

Now he asks magistrate Anne Goldsbrough if he can 'be so bold as to seek another adjournment'. There have been delays in receiving the reports and, mindful of the suspended sentence and seeking to highlight 'exceptional circumstances', he is reluctant to proceed without them. He says one doctor had told him 'incarceration would be detrimental to his [Cook's] mental health'.

The magistrate agrees to hear the case in May. She tells Cook he is free to go.

'Keep up the good work, Your Honour,' he says, raising laughs around the bench. And with that, the old showman emerges: Cook smiles, rises to his full height, puffs out his chest and heads for the door with the swagger so often seen at VFA grounds.

Thirty minutes later, Cook and Balmer have coffee across the road from the court. Balmer, often described as a 'knockabout' criminal lawyer and with a client list including Mark 'Chopper' Read and Mick Gatto, first represented the former football champion in the late 1980s. He remembers it vividly. Facing drug charges, Cook was given a good behaviour bond. 'Your Honour, you can give me a bond for the next twenty years because I won't be coming back to court,' he told the judge.

But since then he's had to call on 'Bernie The Attorney' at least once a year. Balmer regards him more as a friend than a client — they talk two or three times a week, even when he's not in trouble — and he has taken on his latest driving offence on a pro bono basis. Cook is promising to 'sling you some money down the track.' But the lawyer isn't exactly factoring it into his end-of-financial-year accounts. When people speak to him about Cook and observe he's led a remarkable life, Balmer corrects them. 'Mate, he's led three lives.'

ı|||ı

WHEN you mention Fred Cook to people who haven't seen him for a while, they invariably respond with a question: 'How is Freddie?'

You suspect they really want to ask, 'Is he off drugs?' They are pleased to hear he hasn't used for a few years. Cook was on amphetamines for more than two decades. He has long been removed from the lifestyle he enjoyed as a football and media figure and the proprietor of the Station Hotel in Port Melbourne.

When old friends saw him after his slide it was usually on the TV news, after he had been arrested or dealt with in court. He was inhabiting a world they didn't recognise and they felt powerless to pull him away from its orbit.

Yet affection for him has never wavered. People who know him well speak of a sociable man who was always generous with his time and money at the peak of his popularity. They acknowledge his flaws and foibles — his self-destructive streak and tendency to take things to excess, an ability to sniff a short-cut and an immaturity apparent when he casually sprinkles his female conquests into conversation (his wife, Sally Desmond, says he's sixty-six going on fifteen; his sister Pam says he never grew up). But they describe him as a 'loveable larrikin' or 'scallywag' or 'likeable rogue' with a capacity to lighten the mood around him. They wish only the best for him.

'Mate, I wasn't saddened by what happened to Freddie. I was heartbroken,' says his former school mate and Footscray teammate

Ricky Spargo. 'Such a lovely bloke and to see him go down like that ... We all loved the bloke. My mum's 101 and she's loved him all her life, like my old man [former Footscray player Bob Spargo] did.'

He can barely talk about Cook's post-football life. 'Nah, can't cop it. That wasn't my Freddie.'

Spargo was thrilled to learn Cook was doing okay. He hasn't seen him for a long time, but thinks of him often and always fondly. He doubts there is a bad bone in his body.

Balmer holds the same opinion. He says Cook did and still does put friends first. 'Nothing he's been through has knocked that quality out of him,' he says. 'He looks out for others more than he looks out for himself, and as a consequence of that he's left himself destitute. And it's sad, just tragic.'

Former Port Melbourne coach Gary Brice was devastated as he watched Cook's life unravel. He speaks about him with the warmth that football coaches reserve for players who won them premierships. Cook played in three flags under Brice.

'It was a disappointing period of his life. Very disappointing,' he says. 'Hopefully he's got it under control, because I guess with that sort of addiction you never get over it. It's something you have to live with and manage through your life.'

Cook is living on the Mornington Peninsula, where he headed with his future wife Sally Desmond after he was arrested for drug offences for the first time, in 1986.

But he cannot tell a redemption story, a tale of emerging stronger from a wretched experience. It's a daily struggle to stay clean. He has said it hundreds of times: 'I didn't use yesterday, I haven't used today and I probably won't use tomorrow.'

If someone produced white powder, a spoon and a clean needle and told him he could use with no consequences, away he'd go, jabbing his arm as quickly as he could. But he knows the consequences only too well.

In the beginning he took speed to keep up with his many commitments, time management in powder form. A few months earlier he had been asked to retire from Port Melbourne, his footballing home for fourteen years. He says now that drugs were his way of substituting the surge of adrenaline that came from kicking hundreds of goals and winning premierships.

It's a familiar tale: a feted sportsman losing his way after his career ended and the cheering had stopped. Few fell as far or spectacularly as Fred Cook. In his later years, when he should have been speaking about his career or commenting on football affairs, he was trotted out to talk about criminal figures, including Kath Pettingill for the special *The Mother of Evil.* He told how she marked one lot of foils green (for amphetamines) and others red (for heroin) when her son Dennis Allen was shifting drugs at a furious rate in Richmond in the 1980s.

Allen had money falling out of his pockets then. Cook says he would be equally flush if he had a dollar for every time he'd been told he had the world at his feet — and squandered it. 'Pissed it away,' is how he puts it. His regret runs deep, but he tries to suppress it, thinking he'd go mad if he brooded over his many mistakes. Besides, he says, it's hard enough to deal with the present, let alone the past.

ıllı

COFFEE and conversation with Balmer drained, Cook returns to the Ministry of Housing property he has occupied for seven years, a run-down three-bedroom house. The rent is $100 a week. When times were good it wouldn't have served as a backyard shed for the spread he had in Dendy Street, Brighton, one of Melbourne's most exclusive suburbs.

'They'll demolish it soon,' Cook says, opening the front door. 'Well, hopefully they'll demolish it. Have a look at the joint.'

It reeks of neglect. He will not be sad when he has to move out, but he will miss the space it affords him to store his children's possessions. All manner of goods have piled up in the front bedroom.

The red four-door Nissan Pulsar he was driving when police pulled him over twelve months earlier is parked in the driveway. He bought it from a dealer from nearby Hastings for $700 with twelve months' registration and says he hasn't checked the water or oil for a year. 'I put some air in the tyres last week, but that's about it,' he says. 'I've bought a few cars off this guy. As I said to him, they all broke down and it was about time he sold me a good one. It goes, I suppose.'

A well-groomed Malamute dog named Chewie and two cats hover around Cook as he sits and talks animatedly. His tongue was always turbo-charged, stories gushing out of him like a tap. Trapping them is like trying to catch sunlight in a jar. He leaves a lot unfinished before launching into another.

Sally Desmond, from whom he's been separated since 2004, apparently asked him to look after the dog for a few days. 'That was six years ago and she's still here,' Cook laughs, lighting up a cigarette. 'Can't get rid of her. Can't stop her eating the cat food either.' But he admits he likes to have the animals around.

Cook lives quietly, drawing an aged-pension every fortnight and trying to make it last. Sometimes he will buy two cans of Bourbon and Coke or a beer. But he has to stretch every cent.

A year earlier he was better off. He was working on the big Peninsula Link roads project, counting trucks and jotting down registrations as they came and went with landfill. Taking home about $2200 a week, he could slip something to the youngest of his seven children.

'You know how it is. "Dad, I need a new phone. Dad, I need my nails done." So what do you say? You say, "How much do you want?"'

Before the Peninsula extension he did general labour on the Eastlink road development, and drove an earth-moving truck when the Mount Martha Cove Marina was under construction.

The physical work explains why he looks reasonably fit. But he says he's on a 'bucket' of medication, mainly for a heart condition and high cholesterol. It can leave him lethargic. He also suspects it contributes to his mood swings. He will be happy for a week, then overcome by sadness for a day or two. He says he can distinguish between sadness and depression, and he never feels depressed.

Cook likes to have an early breakfast — toast and coffee, and two cigarettes — and watch the ABC News 24 station on the shiny, large flat-screen television in the lounge. News and documentaries hold his interest.

Surprisingly, for a man known to have a leviathan eye for the ladies, he says he'll take female company as it comes.

He's committed only to doing as he pleases. 'I'll go down to Tasmania and propose to Bob Brown before I get married again! I'm used to doing it my way. I'll get out of bed when I'm ready. Cook a steak when I feel like it. Have no-one to tell me to piss off outside to smoke. Whatever suits me.'

Cook speaks to his three children with Desmond — Jarryd, Jordan and Jaimee — most days, and often natters with his great mate Newman. They were opponents on the field and clicked like Lego pieces off it. He concludes every phone call to Newman, as he does most people, with the words, 'Love ya, see ya, bye'. And when he calls people he knows well and will laugh off his bullshit, he'll often greet them with, 'Fred Cook, superstar, here.'

Now and then he catches up with old pals. A few days in to 2014, he had lunch with Balmer and retired sports journalist Scot Palmer at Sorrento. A month later he shared a beer with former Richmond players Tony Jewell and Mal Brown.

'But honestly, I don't get out much. I sit around watching the TV. Watch too much of the bloody thing. I'm going to have to get off my arse and do some exercise. Went and had my heart checked and they put me on one of those treadmills. I could only stay on it for seven minutes and ten seconds!'

Even when he was in his physical prime he wasn't much of a runner. At Port Melbourne he stayed close to the goals, living on his marking. All his former teammates say it: he was a lousy kick, but he had the best hands you'd see on a footballer. The ball got lost in them.

There is little in the house to indicate Cook was a football great. No trophies or premiership medals are on display. He's unsure what happened to them.

A 1970s poster promoting the VFA as the cradle of community football is taped to a lounge room wall. A fit, strong and smiling Cook stands in the front row, his first son Nathan at his feet. He recognises Sandringham's Terry Wilkins and Prahran's Kim Smith as among the other players in the poster.

But ample reminders of the days when he ruled VFA goal squares can be found in the worn blue suitcase he keeps. A fading Ansett baggage tag hangs off the handle. When Cook was on drugs he jumped frog-like from house to house. But he always took the suitcase with him.

Cook opens it to show a few yellowing newspaper clippings, a handful of VFA Recorders, photographs and a falling-apart scrapbook he believes was maintained by a sister. Pieced together, it marks his rise from Footscray Tech Old Boys to league club Footscray, his controversial transfer to Yarraville in the VFA, an equally headline-taking move to Port Melbourne, his many triumphs in Borough red and blue, and his drug-fuelled demise.

It also has evidence of his time as a media man. Newman, Cook, footballer writer Greg Hobbs and ex-Carlton rover Adrian 'Gags' Gallagher are splashed on the front page of the mid-week edition of the pink-papered *Sporting Globe* of 29 March 1978.

'Here's our team,' the *Globe* trumpets. Cook is described as the 'prolific Port Melbourne goalkicker and VFA's biggest drawcard'.

Cook snaps the suitcase shut and points out what he calls his most prized possession from football. It's a small medal that hangs off a long screw on a doorframe in the kitchen.

It was awarded to him in 2007 for serving as an assistant coach and goal umpire for the Kangaroo Flat Primary School side that won a lightning premiership in Bendigo. Jaimee, his youngest child and third daughter, played in the team.

'It would be nice to win one game,' Cook remembers the school sports master telling him before the first match.

'I said to him, "Stuff that, let's win every game." Wouldn't believe it but they won six out of six and finished up with the premiership. Could have cried, I was so proud.' He left the presentation with the words made famous by his childhood hero and adult pal Teddy Whitten: 'We stuck it up 'em!'

He was similarly proud when son Jarryd came second in a league best and fairest on the Peninsula. That year they were living together in a caravan and Cook was still doing drugs. He was so broke he sometimes went to service stations to steal sandwiches for his boy to take to school for lunch. They often used to joke that when the world ended they'd be the only survivors to keep the cockroaches company.

Cook has little interest in big football, regarding it as a 'sheila's game' with a defensive element that bores him. 'Can't be bothered with it. Years ago there was room for everyone: the superstars, the chubby kid who knew how to get the ball, the thugs. They stuffed all that up. Same with how they play. What's wrong with kicking it long down the guts?'

Like many old VFA followers, he barely recognises its replacement, the VFL, a blend of traditional association clubs and AFL reserves teams.

The golden years of a competition he helped make so popular have long passed. But he's pleased that Port Melbourne, after alignments with the Sydney Swans and North Melbourne, has survived as a stand-alone entity. He mingled with players and supporters after Port's grand final victory over Williamstown in 2011. The team went through the season unbeaten, something that was beyond the great Borough sides Cook served.

For a long time Cook stayed away from Port out of embarrassment. He thought his drug use and stints in prison brought shame to a club he loved and was proud to call his footballing home. But now he gets to one or two games a season and is on the mailing list for the past players' newsletter. He mostly stays in touch with Brice and premiership teammates Tony Ebeyer and Billy Swan.

Mention of Swan has him dusting off memories of the 1976 grand final. Famously, Dandenong defender Allan Harper decked Cook after he got on the end of a Swan kick and nonchalantly poked the ball through the goals. Wild scenes followed. Intent on retribution,

Port players went flying in at Harper. At the other end of the ground, rugged Borough George Allen put down Dandenong forward Pat Flaherty.

ATV-O commentator Phil Gibbs described the mayhem. 'Cook's been flattened and it's right on! Harper is in trouble. Let's watch this. And another player has been flattened at the other end of the ground! Flaherty's been flattened at the other end! And there's another one down! A trainer's gone down!'

A minute later, Cook, blood pouring from his mouth, waved away the trainers and theatrically raised his hands as if to say, I'm okay, let's get on with it. Cook was never a fighter on the field. He didn't have to be. Port had strong men who could thrash away with the best of them.

Swan has often said to Cook he would have avoided Harper's harpoon if he'd let the ball bounce through the goals.

'Swanny always brings it up,' Cook says. 'Calls me a selfish bastard and says I should have shepherded it through. Blames me for all that shit that went down.'

After watching a clip of the incident on YouTube, Cook stays silent for a few seconds, appearing emotional.

'Just reminiscing,' he says. 'I tell ya, they were fucking good days. Should have been there.'

3

COOK has forgotten much of what went on in his life from the late 1980s. Yet his recollections of his childhood in Yarraville are as clear and warm as a peak-summer day.

He was born on 16 November 1947 and was named after his father, Frederick William Cook. His mother, Shirley, had three children after young Fred: Rodney, Lynette and Pam.

The family lived at 49 Ovens Street, next to the Bluestone Hotel. Fred Cook senior made his trade as a baker at the nearby Tip Top factory. But the hours got to him and he found more money working as a labourer with Commonwealth Fertilisers, bagging it for use on farms. A quiet man, he provided his family with a comfortable existence and took pleasure from a glass of beer, a cigarette, football and a bet on the horses (his eldest son was amazed how his father could rattle off every winner on any recent racing card).

Fred Cook senior was a handy footballer, turning out for Yarraville in the VFA. He believed he could get better, but broke an ankle in a work mishap and never played again.

Footscray Football Club was one of his great loves, and he adored Ted Whitten. With his mate Barry Mitchell, he would take young Fred and Rodney to watch the Bulldogs at the Western Oval, savouring the wins and cursing the losses.

He took no chances with footballer weather, piling on layers of clothes: thermal underwear, singlet, t-shirt, shirt, cardigan, jumper, coat, overcoat. 'You can always take them off,' he would say when his boys chipped him about wearing so much. When the cold and rain hit, he would peel off a jumper or coat to give to his shivering sons.

Fred Cook senior got tickets for the 1961 VFL grand final on the morning of the match, apparently off the local postman. He and his sons set off for the MCG, excited at the thought of the Scraggers winning their second premiership. But Hawthorn, coached by John Kennedy, beat them to it.

'We were crying at the end of the day,' Cook says. 'They called Hawthorn "Kennedy's Commandos". They killed us. Broke our hearts. Ted Whitten played with a bad thigh. Jesus. It was a long trip home.'

Shirley Cook kept the house spotless and was a fine cook, baking apple pies, tarts and other treats every Saturday. She rarely failed to put hearty meals on the table.

The way Fred Cook tells it, his mother was the disciplinarian of the family and impressed on her offspring the need for common courtesies. 'She'd flog me if I did something wrong,' Cook says. 'Understand that was in the era that kids should be seen and not heard.'

He recalls a Saturday when he was about sixteen and had a few friends around. They decided to go out, but his mother insisted he complete his chores. He said they could wait until tomorrow and turned his back on her. The next thing he knew, he was flat on the floor, struggling to breathe. His mother had picked up a heavy garden broom and thrown it javelin-style into his back. He never did go out on that Saturday afternoon.

But he had deep respect and affection for his mother. Cook says she kissed him on the cheek every day when he left for school and always stuck up for her children.

He cites an example. Cook left Footscray Tech after Year 10 to work in a local abattoir for £14 a week. Missing his mates and the football scene, he returned a year later. But he encountered trouble on his first day back.

It was raining when he and Rodney arrived at school. There was no shelter. Fred made for the corridor, but a teacher told him it was an out-of-bounds area until the bell went. Sent to the principal's office, he was unwilling to take his punishment, a flogging with the strap. After all, he'd just spent twelve months alongside tough working men. He wasn't going to cop the strap over something he thought was trivial.

He was expelled and sent home. When he told his mother what had happened, she put on her hat and white gloves, took her bag and caught a bus to the school.

Marching into the principal's office, she said Fred's jumper had cost £5, she didn't want it soaked by rain and the school wouldn't be expelling him. Pointing to her son, she said, 'You, get off to class'. That was the end of the matter.

Fred Cook remembers family outings after his father got around to buying a car. His mother would pack a picnic lunch and they would spend days at the beach, often meeting aunts, uncles and cousins.

'A very ordinary, working-class, happy family,' Pam Cook, ten years younger than Fred, says. 'We didn't have any tragedies or anything like that. All very normal, really.'

The Cooks ensured their eldest son attended St Lukes Church of England in Yarraville. Young Fred also went to 'CEBS' — the Church of England Boys Society — on Wednesday nights, evening song on Friday nights and Sunday school followed by mass.

His earliest schooling was at Francis Street Primary School, No. 1501. He can still reel off the names of his teachers: Miss Hogan, Miss Short, Miss Gray, Mr Henderson, Mr Crawford and Mr Hick.

But unlike his brother and sisters, he was no great student. He envied their ability in the classroom. For him, the best thing about school was seeing his mates and playing sport. He had his first game of football for the primary school, donning its red and yellow jumper, and says he barely touched the ball.

He was named on a half back and was unfamiliar with the position. 'Just go and stand over there, son,' the coach told him.

Cook got more serious about football when he went to Footscray Tech. He could see that good players received kudos and credit from not only teachers and students, but the wider community. It set him thinking about the possibilities of the game. He started to sleep with a football. 'If you played okay, you suddenly had a bit of clout around the place,' he says.

On Wednesdays, Cook lined up for Tech and on Saturdays for amateur club Footscray Tech Old Boys, where he would be coached by 1954 Footscray premiership player Arthur Edwards. He tried out for the Old Boys Under 17 team as a thirteen-year-old and was rebuffed. The next year he was initially picked on the bench or asked to be goal umpire, but eventually he found a place in the team.

The Old Boys won a grand final at Windy Hill, but Cook was quiet. 'I didn't make a mistake — only because I didn't get a touch,' he recalls. 'At the start of the last quarter the ball came over the pack and I grabbed it and I ran in to the goals. I kicked it right through the middle — of the points. There was no interchange in those days. I just got dragged.'

Cook senior went into the rooms and told his son he might as well go home, hammer a four-inch nail in the chook shed and hang his boots from it. 'You've got to find a sport you can play. It's not football,' he said.

If that sounds harsh, Cook says his father watched every game he played and took pleasure from his many accolades and achievements. They were photographed together after Cook won the 1970 J. J. Liston Trophy after his mark-filled season for Yarraville. Fred Cook senior's eyes shine with filial pride.

Fred junior's football began to take off when he was sixteen. He grew six inches and his many kick-to-kick sessions with his mates on the streets of Yarraville refined his marking and kicking.

He won a club and competition best and fairest at Under 17 level. Soon scouts from Footscray were running an eye over him. It eventually led to an invitation to a training session. And there he was introduced to his idol, E. J. Whitten. Cook was so nervous he stammered, 'Pleased to meet you, Mr Whitten.'

'Well, it was like going to church and finding God at the altar,' Cook says. 'He was a man amongst men.'

In his first year back at Footscray Tech, Cook was threatened with expulsion a second time after being caught smoking in the toilets. But because of his football ability he was encouraged to sign a sorry book and forget about it. 'They didn't want me to miss any games,' he says. 'Actually, we were in the Victorian Inter-Tech grand final at the number one oval at Albert Park. We won it.'

Ricky Spargo and Norm Mitchell, both destined to play league football at Footscray, played in the team, as did John Sharp, a future VFA player with Yarraville and star District cricketer with Footscray. Teammates carried Spargo from the ground as he showed off the handsome trophy.

Spargo says the team had a simple game plan: kick it long to 'Freddie' in the goal square.

'We couldn't go wrong,' he says. 'We were actually behind in that game, but Freddie took over. No-one could stop him. Game over. He was the best mark of a football you could see. Don't think I saw the bugger drop one. Best hands I've ever seen in football.'

Spargo and Cook met at the Technical school and became great friends. They had a lot in common. 'Freddie was like me,' Spargo says. 'He was a bit wilder than me, but he loved life. He was always up. He was always happy. And he had a big mouth!

'You wouldn't meet a better bloke. I would have killed for him. Geez, I've got some great memories of Freddie.'

Pam Cook says her brother was fortunate to discover he was an exceptional footballer.

'Wouldn't we all love to find that one thing in life that we're really good at and can excel at? He found that.'

When his hands weren't holding a football, Cook was known to put them to mischievous use, breaking into factories and stealing cars. He insists the vehicles were never knocked around and that he always dumped them outside police stations.

When he needed a few bob he stole soft drinks from the back of a local fish and chip shop, and took them around the front and sold them.

'It was typical teenage-boy stuff,' Cook says. 'No harm done, really.'

But police took a dimmer view of his behaviour and more than once brought him home to his startled parents. They were dismayed by their son's casual regard of the law. The indifference never left him.

He first appeared in court in June 1963 for 'factory break and steal' and 'illegal use of motor car', receiving probation for seventy-eight weeks. In March 1965, he was up for 'larceny from motor vehicle'. He was given a good behaviour bond.

When he was about fourteen, Cook and his mates dug a tunnel in the soft, sandy soil of the banks of the Yarra River, covered it with railway sleepers and canvas, and went about filling it with stolen goods for which they ultimately had no use. When a security guard from an oil company came across the lair and reported it to police, *The Sun* newspaper dubbed the unknown gang 'The River Pirates'.

A few years earlier, Cook and Rodney stumbled upon two children who had gone missing in Yarraville. The brothers had jumped the fence of the Tip Top factory to take the delivery vans for a spin. Climbing into the self-locking vehicle, they found the frightened youngsters, a boy, five, and a girl, four, huddling in the back.

When police arrived, the Cooks thought they would be in trouble for trespassing. But they were praised for rescuing the children.

'If it wasn't for my brother being mischievous, they would probably have died,' Pam Cook says.

Under the headline 'Children Trapped 30 Hours In Van', *The Sun* newspaper reported the incident, quoting a ten-year-old 'Freddy' Cook as telling the boy: 'You'd better get home. He told me faintly, "I think I'd better."'

It was the first of many times that Fred Cook was held up as a hero.

4

WITHIN Fred Cook's battered blue suitcase are a few large pages long ago torn from a scrapbook. Glued and stapled to the bottom of one is his registration form to play with Footscray. It is dated 11 April 1967 and signed by Cook, Footscray secretary Bill Dunstan and a Victorian Football League director.

Years later, Cook says it's likely his hand was trembling as pen hovered over paper.

He had set his compass on the Western Oval ever since he had started to come through the ranks at Footscray Tech and the amateur club. At age nineteen he was signed and sealed to play under the coaching of the great Charlie Sutton and the captaincy of (in Cook's eyes) the even greater Ted Whitten.

Throughout his teenage years he and a mate, Jeff Chapman, had gone to the Footscray ground once a week to watch the Scraggers train. They'd nick the occasional football, but Cook got a greater thrill stealing a glimpse of his heroes: John Schultz, Ray Baxter, Alex 'Racehorse' Gardiner, Graham and Barry Ion, John Hoiles, Ray Walker, Charlie Evans. And, of course, Whitten, who would ruffle his hair and say, 'G'day kid.' Now he could count a few of his pin-ups as teammates.

And he was another Footscray Tech Old Boy who'd made it to

league football. The club had been rich recruiting territory for the Bulldogs. In 1967, Cook was photographed alongside three other Tech talents kicking on at the Western Oval: Noel Fincher, Rod O'Connor and Gary Dempsey.

'I was probably the happiest young bloke walking the earth, the day I joined that club,' Cook says. 'Excited, elated, achievement, words like that. It was a big thing for me.'

Yet not three years later, after thirty-three senior games and the ability to play many more, he walked out, never to return. A spat with officials turned into a saga played out in the newspapers, and in a huff he made off for Yarraville in the VFA. At twenty-one he'd played his last game of league football. His Old Boys teammate Dempsey went on to captain the club and win the 1975 Brownlow Medal during a glittering 329-match career.

Dempsey says Cook was 'bigger than life even then' and 'didn't like too much discipline'.

'He wasn't that keen on doing everything other people's way,' Dempsey says.' He wanted to do it his way, and when he left Footscray and went to the association he was allowed to play his own footy. At Footscray he had to play a team game.'

Dempsey has no doubt Cook could have been a long-term league player. He considers him a wasted talent.

Another of Footscray's Brownlow Medal-winning ruckmen, John Schultz, agrees. He says league football caught only a glimpse of Cook's ability.

'When you think of how much he had going for him, he should have played many more games,' Schultz says. 'Nothing frightened him. He was rugged and tough. He'd get the ball at centre half back and go straight down the centre and head for goal. No pussy-footing around. He was the sort of bloke you wanted in your team.'

He recalls Cook as a 'loveable larrikin' and 'personable bloke' who was 'always smiling and joshing around'.

Schultz was fond of the youngster. When he retired at the end of the 1968 season, he gifted Cook his aluminium shinguards. Cook never forgot it; when he thinks of John Schultz, he thinks of the shinguards.

Laurie Sandilands, who made his debut for Footscray in 1966 and went on to captain the club, saw a 'larrikin' young player who struggled to handle authority, was a non-conformist and had a 'different attitude to life in general'.

With the amateur season over, Cook and Dempsey first turned out for Footscray in 1966, in a night match against South Melbourne and a reserves game against Collingwood at Collingwood. Cook remembers club secretary Jack Collins dropping by the family home with papers, most probably for a permit, to sign.

Fred Cook senior was initially reluctant for his boy to commit, believing he needed another twelve months in the amateurs. But Collins tempted him with a fistful of finals tickets. He changed his mind.

'I said to the old man, "Hey, I thought you said I wasn't ready for it." And he said, "Fred, you're never too young to play league football. You've got to get in and mix it with them." Tickets for the finals game were like gold that year. You couldn't get them anywhere. But Jack Collins had a few and the old man was happy to take them off him.'

Cook was taken aback at the step-up from amateur to league football. A ball hardly hit the ground at training. Leads were honoured with accurate passes that arrived at speed. Players scooped up balls from their boot laces with ease. Cook soon found himself doing the same.

'Coming from the amateurs, it was like going up three steps in the quality of your football,' he says. 'Early doors, I was overawed. I was. But what happens is, you lift yourself to the standard of the players around you. They dragged me along. You say, "Right, this is how league footballers train," and you get carted along. You eventually get the confidence.'

His time at the Bulldogs began promisingly. Footscray had a wooden-spoon season — fourteen losses crowded out only four victories — but the well-built whipper-snapper played seven senior games, mainly as a defender.

Handed jumper No. 29, he was there for Round 1 of 1967, against reigning premier St Kilda at Moorabbin. A crowd of 28,564 watched the Saints collar the Dogs by eighty-one points. Cook started on the bench. He stood next to Verdun Howell when he went on the ground.

'Howell flogged me. Stood on my head, all those sorts of things,' he says. 'I learnt quickly. You had to.'

But his talent attracted good notices in the newspapers.

'If the performance by nineteen-year-old Fred Cook on Saturday is any criterion, Footscray's worries about finding a regular centre half back have been erased,' kicked off one match report.

'Cook, 6.2 and 13.10, did an excellent job against an accomplished centre half forward in [North Melbourne's] Bernie McCarthy, a feature being his superb overhead marking. He also showed dash and aggression.'

As he rose, Cook encountered for the first time those ubiquitous sporting figures, the hangers-on.

'How you doin' champ?' people would say to him, patting his back and digging fingers into his arms. Suddenly he had a lot more friends. He couldn't pop into the Bluestone Hotel without drinkers coming over and wanting to talk football and buy him a beer. 'Wherever you went everyone seemed to know you,' Cook says.

Suddenly he wasn't Mr Fred Cook. He was Mr Popular. Youngsters asked for autographs. He wondered if he should sign 'Fred Cook' or 'Freddie Cook' and if he should prevail 'best wishes' upon the recipients.

His profile got bigger in 1968. Cook played every senior game that year and stood some of the league's most brilliant forwards, including St Kilda's Darrel Baldock. He remembers Sutton telling him that Baldock was an explosive player and a champion of the game, but he could be frustrated with close checking — and a few kicks in the heel as he set off for the ball. 'So that's what I did, booted him with each and every alternating step,' Cook says. 'What a prick of a thing that was to do.'

Cook worshipped Sutton. 'He encouraged the way I liked to play football,' he says. 'In those days you could put the ball under your arm, run down from centre half back and swing your other arm like a club, a mallet. That was legal. Charlie told me that was the way he wanted me to play. I did.'

That encounter against Baldock was in Round 7 at Moorabbin. Both were named in the best. The great Saint was credited with twenty-four disposals and three goals. Cook had eighteen possessions and seven marks.

In the return match in Round 18, Cook again did well in a match St Kilda again won comfortably. In his round-up for *The Footscray Mail*, Gary Sargeant said Cook was 'the best of a handful of good players' and that his marking was 'the turning point for many St Kilda attacks, but he lacked sufficient support from his fellow defenders to make much difference'.

'In view of the fact that he was carrying a sore elbow his strong marking is even more praiseworthy.'

Sargeant had hailed Cook's performance against Fitzroy three rounds earlier. The Roys' winning margin of five points, he wrote, would have been far greater 'only for the relentless defensive work of Fred Cook at centre half back'.

'Cook was in dazzling touch, scorching around the half back line like a two-year-old. His pace and vigour frustrated Fitzroy thrusts continually. The outstanding feature of his play was undoubtedly his brilliant overhead marking. In the air he was unbeatable, outmarking opponents at every contest. Cook's inspiring leadership of the defence in the second quarter was largely responsible for preventing Fitzroy wrapping up the game at half time.'

Forty-six years later, Dempsey recalls Cook's marking as his outstanding skill. 'He was a shocking kick, worse than me, which is saying something. And he was a worse kick than Barry Round, which is amazing. He couldn't kick it over a jam tin,' Dempsey says. 'But he was a good player. Centre half back. Great hands. Great mark of the football.'

Cook didn't soar to the heights of, say, Carlton aerialist Alex Jesaulenko. But he'd watched the former Australian high jumper Tony Sneazwell train a few times and worked out a method in which he would leap for a mark at the last possible moment, then throw his arms skywards. It worked for him. 'That's one thing I could do, catch it,' he says, remembering that the great football writer Alf Brown once bracketed him with Dempsey, Peter Knights and David 'Swan' McKay as the best marking men in the game. Brown asserted that Cook wasn't as spectacular as Knights or Malcolm Blight 'but he pulls down big ones more consistently'.

Footscray improved marginally in 1968, winning five games, losing fifteen and settling tenth on the ladder, above only Fitzroy and North Melbourne. Sutton finished up as coach at the end of the season and was replaced by Whitten.

In an article in *The Sporting Globe*, Sutton said business pressures and the time needed to coach at VFL level had prompted him to step down. He called Dempsey a 'real up-and-comer'. And he had good things to say about Cook, declaring that he should develop into one of the club's best players. Sutton described him as a 'big, strong dasher' who was unafraid to get in front for a mark and could turn defence into attack.

Cook earned seven Brownlow Medal votes, behind only three other Bulldogs: Schultz (eleven votes), George Bisset (nine votes) and David Thorpe (eight votes). He was judged Footscray's most improved player. And by that stage he had youngsters carrying his bag into the ground. One of them, he says, was Doug Hawkins, later to break Whitten's games record.

Hawkins chortles when the scenario is put to him. 'I may have. I can't honestly remember. But it's a bloody good story anyway.' Referring to his own rise, Hawkins adds, 'But you can say this: twenty years later, Freddie Cook wasn't fit to carry my bag into any football ground!'

The 1969 season didn't begin well for Cook. On a pre-season jaunt to country Victoria he messed with bags on the bus, swapping players' gear around. It was harmless stuff, but five minutes later he himself couldn't see the humour in it. Officials, he says, took a dim view of his antics and 'filed it away for a later date'.

He played the first six senior games of the season, then was dropped.

The way Cook tells it, Sutton, trying to maintain spirits around the club after five consecutive defeats, arranged a get-together at his home the day after the Round 6 defeat against Collingwood. Collins, he says, heard about it and, fearing a booze-up, asked players not to attend. Those who did might be disciplined, he warned.

But Cook went along and was dumped to the reserves the following week against South Melbourne, as were Laurie Sandilands, Gary Merrington, Ivan Marsh and Len Cumming. He stewed.

'Of course I was shitty. I didn't see any harm in going to Charlie's place. It wasn't like I was going there to drink the joint dry,' he says. 'I'd learned to stand up for myself, see, and I wasn't going to let Jack Collins tell me what I could or couldn't do.'

As he slummed it in the reserves, growing more annoyed by the week, Cook got talking to Martin Duggan, who ran the Bluestone Hotel and also supplied beer for a social club, The Grafters, attached to VFA team Yarraville.

Duggan told Cook that Footscray was treating him shabbily by keeping him out of a senior team in which he'd established himself the previous season. How about going to Yarraville for the rest of the season? he asked. You'll be looked after. And you can always go back to the Bulldogs once heads cool. They know you can play. They'll take you back any day.

Cook says Duggan offered him a sign-on of $4000 and a house of his choosing. He would also receive weekly match payments of $90. All he had to do was play out the season at Yarraville and then all of 1970. Where he went after that was up to him.

'My head started spinning. That was a massive package,' Cook recalls. 'And I couldn't say no. I needed the money.'

By that stage Cook was twenty-one, but already married with a child. He'd met Bernadette Dewan at the Hampton Hotel. They wed at St Paul's Catholic Church in Bentleigh in 1968, not long after their daughter Jacqueline was born.

The young family was living in a flat in Hyde Street, Footscray, made vacant when the Bulldogs' South Australian recruit Peter Anderson went home. Cook was working at Walpamur Paints.

'I worked out I had to start looking after myself,' Cook says.

'In 1968 I played twenty home-and-away games, three night games and I was paid $875 for the whole season.'

As he wallowed in the reserves, Richmond came calling. Tigers official Alan Schwab phoned Cook and said the club was keen on him. Cook remembers talk of a swap with Mike Perry.

Footscray's secretary at the time, Bill Dunstan, told *Footscray Advertiser* reporter Roy Jamieson, 'A Richmond official phoned me late last week. We talked about Sunday football and then about other things. Then he asked me, "What is the position with Fred Cook?" I told him, "You have got to be joking." I said that Cook had been dropped to the reserves because he had lost a bit of form, but it probably would not be long before he got his form back and was returned to the senior team.'

But Cook was less convinced of his senior prospects. He was no fan of Collins and believed his spell in the reserves had to do with issues other than football. He thought he'd played well in one reserves match, only to be deflated when a member of the match committee assessed his performance as 'just fair'.

He made up his mind: he would buy the house Duggan had dangled and he would go to Yarraville. He and Bernadette took a fancy to a three-bedroom weatherboard with nice gardens in Pitt Street, West Footscray, clinching it for $9700 from the Farnbach Burnham real estate agency.

'All of a sudden at twenty-one years of age I'm sitting in my own home,' Cook says. 'Even the rates were paid for me. Hey, I'm on Easy Street.'

On 6 June, *The Age* and *Sun* newspapers reported Cook had walked out on the Bulldogs and was headed for the VFA without a clearance.

Cook told *Age* man Peter McFarline he'd played poorly against Collingwood, but his earlier performances had him leading the club voting on Channel 7's *World of Sport* program.

He mentioned the Sunday get-together at Sutton's home, pointing out that nine of the eleven players who attended had been dropped.

'I received a very good offer from Yarraville. It helped my wife, child and myself into a home, and it was too good to turn down.'

In an interview with *The Footscray Advertiser*, Cook said the committee had told him he had to 'curb my "mannerism" around the club and to direct it in a way that would help the club'. He said, 'But it has always been my nature to speak to people as I find them. I would rather say something to a man's face than go behind his back and tell someone else.'

Shortly after Cook's walk-out, Collins declared that Sutton was 'not very welcome at the club'. He said the 1954 premiership coach 'had something to do' with the defender defecting to the association.

At the time Cook denied it, but he says Sutton did encourage him to make the move. 'He said to me, "You're not getting a go here, you've got a top offer from Yarraville, you might as well go." Mind you, I had hundreds of advisors. But I couldn't see them picking me again. They dropped me to the seconds as a smartener-upper. They left me there rotting.'

Cook remains adamant he was in contention to play for Victoria, saying a selector had told him it would be embarrassing for all concerned if the state centre half back was plucked from the reserves.

'I was probably the third cab off the rank,' he says, 'but I could have ended up the first because of injuries to others players, namely Peter Walker of Geelong and Peter Steward of North Melbourne.'

Did he put his grievances to his coach? It would have made no difference, he says, because Whitten wasn't picking the side.

He went to Whitten's house in Altona and told him he was going. Whitten said he was disappointed, but understood. 'He actually wrote me a letter and told me to pull my head in because I was captaincy material,' Cook says.

Even as he took off to Yarraville he was thinking about a return to league football. But what was shaped as a long and successful career was over.

Sandilands cannot remember Cook's run-in with Collins, but says he wasn't alone in clashing with the secretary. Sandilands also had his differences with Collins. 'Jack was a very hard man to get on with, particularly if he'd had a drink,' he says. 'Freddie had a drink and I had a drink and we weren't Jack's favourite people.'

Sandilands says Cook certainly created an impression at Footscray. 'He was there for 1967, 1968 and a bit of 1969. So the time he spent there was brief, but everyone remembers it.'

Cook's school mate Ricky Spargo finished with sixty-four games for Footscray from 1966 to 1971. He still laughs about the time he was twentieth man in a match and Cook was the nineteenth. Cook had turned up in a terrible state after a night of 'wine, women and song'. The trainers did their best to rouse him for the match ahead. As they watched the play in the second quarter, Cook called over a pie seller and said to Spargo, 'Now, what are you having, a pie or a pastie?' Spargo said he couldn't possibly stomach either. Cook gulped down a pie and washed it down with a can of Coke.

'True story,' Spargo says. 'That day they actually found him asleep at the club. The bugger hadn't been to bed from the night before.'

John Schultz says it was a shame Cook's time at the Western Oval ended so suddenly, believing Footscray could have used him for many years.

Schultz chuckles as he recalls kicking and marking practice that pitted he and Murray Zeuschner at one end and fellow big men Cook and Dempsey at the other.

Zeuschner was a dedicated footballer and desperate to prove himself a senior player. He made Schultz fight for every mark. Schultz figured that if he could get through such spirited training sessions on Thursday nights, he could get through matches on Saturday afternoons. But there was no such fierce competition at the other end. The new chums waxed.

'Here we are going very hard indeed and the other two were taking it in turns to take marks!' Schultz says. 'They were lackadaisical, both of them. They were just going through the motions. They had so much talent, but at that stage they didn't realise it. The penny dropped with Gary and he became a real star, won his six best and fairests. But maybe Fred didn't understand what he had.'

Yarraville, then coached by 1958 Collingwood premiership player John Henderson, quickly understood what it had: an exceptional player. Cook helped the Eagles to a 9–9 season, being named in the best in ten of his eleven games. In his first match in the VFA, he lined up in the ruck and slotted five goals in a narrow defeat against Dandenong.

Jim 'Frosty' Miller played in the match for Dandy. By the time they finished their VFA careers Cook and Miller had more than 2000 goals between them — and lasting fame in the Victorian game.

5

THE voting for the J. J. Liston Trophy, the award for the VFA's best and fairest player, reflected Fred Cook's impact at Yarraville in 1970.

The Eagles had a poor season, winning only one game, finishing on the bottom of the ladder and being relegated to Division 2. Yet Cook won the Liston. Well, he didn't win — he streaked it in, polling forty-one votes to defeat the runner-up, Williamstown's former Footscray player Kevin Jackman, by fourteen in the count at VFA House. He was overlooked for votes in only four games.

Cook celebrated his victory at the Yarraville clubrooms, where teammates were photographed hoisting the sideburned and suited star on their shoulders. Footscray great Charlie Sutton, driving home from his Yarraville hotel, dropped in to offer congratulations.

Cook had paid for the shindig using money won in player awards tallied by the local paper. 'That was the done thing. Any coin you picked up you put towards a piss-up for the players.'

Cook turned up late, not wanting to leave home until he found out he'd won. His father phoned to confirm his victory.

He had entered the count as one of the favourites after a season in which he averaged almost twenty-seven kicks and fourteen marks a match. He was credited with forty-one kicks against Dandenong and he had between twenty-seven and thirty-seven in nine other games.

His performance against Dandy had football scribe Wal Bright praising him to the skies. Cook 'practically took Dandenong on single-handed only to see his team well beaten by 63 points,' Bright wrote in an article headlined 'Cook gets 41 kicks — but Eagles downed'.

'Cook had the phenomenal tally of 41 kicks and 20 marks,' Bright wrote. 'He spent the four quarters at the wind-assisted end of the ground. He was the loose man when Dandenong had the breeze, then spent the other two terms in the forward zone.'

Bright also watched a 35-kick effort against Port Melbourne. Cook took on his future teammates Vic 'Stretch' Aanensen and Brendan Behan, and brought in eighteen marks.

John Heriot, a fine backman for South Melbourne over 153 games and full back of its team of the century, coached Yarraville in 1970. Now seventy-four and a lifelong resident of Spotswood, Heriot says Cook was the stand-out player of the season, and the Liston could have gone to no-one else. 'Freddie wasn't the strongest kick, but he was the best mark of a football you'd ever see. Wouldn't find a bloke with a better pair of hands,' he says, echoing the words of Gary Dempsey and many others.

'I played him on the ball,' Heriot says. 'I always agreed with the theory that if you've got a good player you stick him on the ball, not in a position, and let him run around. That's what I did with Freddie, gave him his head to win the ball as much as he possibly could. And he really dominated some games. It's just a pity we didn't have too many other good players around him.'

Alan Bongetti, who played at Yarraville from 1967 to 1971, remembers being taken aback at the news that Cook would be joining the club from Footscray. Bongetti immediately thought the Eagles had themselves an outstanding player — and Cook exceeded his expectations.

'Beautiful footballer,' he says. 'As far as marking the football, just tremendous. Every time the ball went near him he'd just mark it. It was a joy to play with someone who had that ability, really.'

Cook quips that every time he kicked the ball at Yarraville he knew it was coming back 'quick smart'. The club had some good players, he says, but not the depth to live with even mid-range teams. 'Honestly, we weren't that bad. But it was a strong comp back then. Prahran won the flag that year. They had the great Kevin Rose coaching them. There weren't any easy kicks in first division.'

As for that 41-kick performance against Dandenong, he says he had a row with Bernadette the night before the match and skulked off to drown his sorrows. One drink became many, and by Sunday morning he was feeling rough. He phoned Heriot and said it might be best if he sat that game out. Heriot said that was fine, but he should turn up to support his teammates.

When Cook arrived, the coach told him, 'Strip — we've rearranged the side and we need you to ruck all day.'

When he became ill during the match, Cook told the Yarraville trainer he'd eaten a corned beef and chutney sandwich that didn't agree with him.

'Forty-one kicks after I hadn't been to bed. Everyone's entitled to a bad day now and then,' Cook says with a laugh.

Apart from the J. J. Liston Trophy, he also won Yarraville's best and fairest and, in a media award, a $2000 boat, which he put to use at Melton Reservoir and Pykes Creek.

Soon he was testing other waters. Cook had fulfilled his

obligations with Yarraville, but for a time said he would be staying with the Eagles.

'The club helped me when I was down, so I will be sticking by it,' he told *The Footscray Advertiser*. 'I'm very happy at Yarraville — they're a terrific club.' He even said he hoped to coach the Eagles one day.

But Cook had no desire to play in Division 2. During the season there had been talk that another VFL club, noting Cook's undimmed brilliance in the VFA, would target him in 1971.

In crossing from Footscray to Yarraville, Cook broke the VFL's clearance laws and automatically picked up a twelve-month ban. He would have to stand out of football for a year to earn the right of appeal against his disqualification.

Still, he considered trying to salve old wounds and return to Footscray, at one point even working under professional running coach Cliff Pryde. He also lifted weights four times a week at the Sunshine Sports Club.

Then came an approach from Port Melbourne. Its legendary administrator Norm Goss had seen Cook dominate for Yarraville, and decided the club could do with him.

In fact, Port had tried to filch him when he was in dispute with Footscray in 1969. Bulldog John Jillard told Borough officials that Cook was a fine player, but not always vigilant in picking up his opponent. Goss and fellow official Charlie 'Dooley' Chrimes waited for Cook outside his house, finally giving up at 2am. They left a note expressing their interest and urging him to make contact. They heard nothing back.

But by 1970 things had changed. Yarraville played at Port in the last match of the season, and Goss and Chrimes spoke to Cook after the game.

'I don't want to play in Second Division,' Chrimes remembers Cook telling him when they whisked him to the committee room.

'You won't have to. You'll play here,' Chrimes replied.

Heriot can remember the night Port Melbourne officials visited Yarraville and declared their intention to sign the J. J. Liston Trophy champion.

'They said they could pay him a lot of money. And we didn't have the bagful of money they had. Simple as that. I said to them, "He's all yours, because we can't afford that." And off he went. And what a career he had there.'

Cook says the Port offer wasn't over the top — 'they gave me a couple of thousand and said they'd pay me $90 a game' — and his switch of clubs was more about staying in the top division.

Carrying a transfer fee of $1500, Borough committeeman Ray Downard went to a butcher's shop in Yarraville to complete the deal. Eagles secretary Bill Curwood was reluctant to release his club's best player, but he signed the clearance form on a butcher's block.

Chrimes, eighty-one, says $1500 was a lot of money at the time, but it was one of the best investments Port ever made. 'When you think of what he achieved, he was worth every cent, I tell you right now,' he says. 'To me, he was a great clubman and an extraordinary player. He hardly gave us a bad game.'

Cook disliked Port Melbourne almost as much as he did Collingwood. But he had great respect for it and was keen to play in a successful side. 'I held them in awe. Everyone was shit-frightened of playing against them because they were so tough. Don't worry, they had some tough men in that side.'

Heriot was like many football followers in the 1970s: he took pleasure in watching Cook pile up the goals for Port Melbourne. He doubts the Borough would have won so many flags without him.

As Cook crossed the river, beginning an association with Port that would bring him more than a decade of unceasing success, hard times hovered over Yarraville.

The 1970 season was its last in the VFA's first division, although it did make grand finals in 1977 (under the coaching of former Bulldog David Thorpe) and in 1980 (when coached by future North Melbourne premiership mentor Denis Pagan).

Prominent Melbourne youth worker Les Twentyman steered the Eagles in 1981, and the short-fused John Sharp was in charge in 1982. But dogged by debt and a lack of sponsors, Yarraville dropped out of the VFA shortly before the 1984 season. Its identity was revived when Kingsville changed its name to Yarraville in 1996 and there was a merger with Seddon in 2007.

The Yarraville Seddon website has a history section. And in a photograph representing the period of 1961 to 1976, there is Fred Cook, arms extended high as he follows through on a kick, a glorious image of the club's last J. J. Liston Trophy winner.

6

FRED Cook started at Port Melbourne in 1971. By the time he finished in 1984, he'd become a towering figure at the Borough and in the VFA, a full forward who was as popular as he was prolific in front of the goals.

He topped the century seven times on his way to 1236 goals, featured in six premierships, captained the club and Victoria, won a best and fairest, and made a record 253 appearances.

He had turned his back on league football, unwisely, thought people in a good position to judge. But his public profile would soar in the VFA and eventually exceed those of many VFL players.

Cook seemed to be everywhere: on Channel 7's *World of Sport*, reading out the teams at radio station 3DB, and writing for *The Sporting Globe* and *The Sunday Press*. He was also a regular on the sportsman's night circuit, often accompanied by his pal Sam Newman. They'd turn up, tell a few funny stories and answer some questions. And they'd leave with a few beers under their belts and a few hundred dollars in their pockets.

Few players could land a page 1 photo on the big-selling *Sun News-Pictorial*, as Cook did in 1978. He had visited a kindergarten in East Bentleigh, and snaps of the burly footballer in full playing gear mixing with the littlies made for a spread in the middle-pages: 'Fred shows 'em how'.

Flamboyant from top to toe, he was a poster boy for the association, bringing it untold publicity. The VFA made it official when it put him on the payroll as a promotions officer, with executive director Keith Mills saying Cook was as well known among junior footballers as Alex Jesaulenko and Kevin Sheedy.

In a competition crowded with hard men, he bunched his fists only to celebrate his goals (he went through his long career without being reported). Cook had more than enough teammates who could ping away punches when things got willing. The archetypal Borough was as fearless as he was ferocious.

'Fred Cook was more of a matinee idol than a football star,' sports writer Garry Linnell said of Cook in 1990. 'It seemed he was there on television every Sunday afternoon, taking a big grab, kicking a match-winning goal.'

Some veteran supporters dared to mention him in the same breath as Port's legendary 1950s All Australian ruckman Frank Johnson, who went to South Melbourne late in his career and won the best and fairest in his first season.

As for younger fans, they wore Cook's No. 5 on their blue and red jumpers, and thrilled at his every exploit. At siren's end they would besiege him with pens and paper, and he took care to give autographs to all of them. He knew some were from battling families. Football was their weekly highlight and he was their hero. Cook arranged for a printer to run off hundreds of copies of his photograph in his Port Melbourne jumper. He would write a personalised message for any boy or girl seeking his signature.

Alan Wickes, president of the VFA from 1981 to 1984, noticed how well Cook treated his fans, stoking his popularity. When he thinks of Cook, he pictures him on the ground ten minutes after games, signing youngsters' jumpers.

'There were a lot of little No. 5s out there,' Wickes says. 'But Cookie looked after them. When he was signing for a kid he was probably talking to the dad as well. And that's a very humane thing, isn't it? That's why he was so loved. That was Fred. He wanted to please everybody — but that was probably his weakness.'

After one match, Cook left the field bloodied from a frustrated full back's fist. His father arranged for him to be stitched. 'The doctor's ready,' he said, motioning him to the rooms. But Cook was surrounded by dozens of young fans. He couldn't let them down. 'How can I walk away from this? Tell the doc to wait a bit,' he said.

More than a few single mothers asked Cook to have a quiet word with their rebellious sons. When he did, their behaviour invariably improved. One lad, who had been refusing to attend school, was startled when his idol turned up at his door and told him it was important he put time into his studies. Picking up his bag, off he went.

At one stage, Cook earned the sobriquet 'Kissing Fred'. It started when he began greeting his daughters with a peck on the lips as he came off the ground. Soon other littlies were lining up for a smooch. 'It is like a visit from royalty with Fred bestowing kisses, smiles and head-pats all-round,' wrote *The Herald*'s Alf Brown.

Port Melbourne didn't have to wait to see Cook at his best when he crossed from Yarraville. Under the coaching of former champion Borough forward Bob Bonnett, the recruit polled twenty-four votes to finish fifth in the J. J. Liston Trophy, five behind the winner, Preston's former Collingwood player Laurie Hill.

Playing all eighteen games, mostly at centre half back, he was second to Jim Buckley in the club best and fairest. Norm Goss junior, who would go on to be a first-class league rover, was third.

But the Borough dropped from third in 1970 to sixth in 1971. Bonnett retired at season's end. The club's annual report noted he 'did his utmost to bring success to the club, but his efforts to win games, at times, fell on deaf ears. It was certain to all supporters that if his instructions had been heeded at all times Port could have easily finished in the final four'. The club hired tenacious 1968 Carlton premiership player Ian Collins to replace him.

Although he had despised it, Cook immediately felt at home at Port Melbourne. Teammates became mates. Supporters smarted over defeats, but were loyal, slapping his back on days good and bad. Mostly, they were good, and it was common for diehards to thrust money into Cook's hand after games.

After he had performed well in one match, an old-timer on a walking frame inched towards him in the rooms. 'I thought you played well today, Fred,' he said, passing him $2. Cook told him to save it for a day when he played poorly. The next week, after Cook found kicks elusive, the supporter reappeared and stabbed the money into his hand. He has never forgotten it.

'Once you put on that jumper, you were part of a family, the Port Melbourne family,' he says. 'I actually felt like I'd been adopted. Mind you, plenty of people reminded me you weren't a local until you'd put in ten good years. It was a different time back then. Port had the firsts, the seconds, the thirds and the fourths, and if you were a kid growing up in Port Melbourne and you had a bit of ability, you wanted to play football for Port Melbourne. And, by geez, when they got there they'd do anything to win. That's what made the club so strong. They played for the jumper, right up to the final bell. And Old Man Goss [Norm Goss] looked after everyone.'

Premiership men including Gary Brice, Bob 'Bullwinkle' Profitt, Graeme 'Arms' Anderson, Vic 'Stretch' Aanensen, Graham 'Buster' Harland, David 'Sam' Holt, Billy Swan and Greg 'Biff' Dermott were examples of locals rising to senior ranks and becoming distinguished servants. Brownlow Medal champion Peter Bedford was another.

Brice grew up in Liardet Street, so close to the North Port Oval that he could hear the roar of the crowd on Sundays. He watched Port most weeks and Bonnett was his idol. When mates at school asked him which team he supported, he always said Port Melbourne, not a league side. He started playing for the Port seconds in 1966, after his secondary schooling. Bonnett was captain and coach of the team. Brice had an outstanding league career at South Melbourne and steered the Borough to the 1980, 1981 and 1982 premierships, but he says playing alongside Bonnett was a highlight of his career.

'What Fred says is exactly right,' Brice says. 'It was ingrained in all the kids in Port Melbourne — that was the club to be at. We were in South Melbourne's zone but they weren't having a lot of success, so it was always a case of, if you were going to play good football, you were going to go to Port Melbourne. It was a burning ambition of mine to do it.'

When Cook and other players talk of their time at Port, they invariably speak with affection and admiration for Norm Goss.

Watching football at North Port Oval, you take a seat in the Norm Goss grandstand. It overlooks a ground with a white picket fence and carries the eye to surrounding factories, and beyond them a glimpse of Melbourne's skyline.

The grandstand is named after a man who served Port with

tenacity as a player and with distinction as a straight-talking administrator who put the club's interests above all else. The ground was his second home; if he wasn't at the family residence in Clark Street (where he and his wife, Lillian, raised nine children), he was at the club.

Norm Goss played in Port Melbourne's 1940 and 1941 premierships, alongside Tommy Lahiff, with whom he formed a lasting friendship. Lahiff took over as coach of the Port team after the resignation of Frank Kelly shortly before the 1941 finals. Up against Coburg in the decider, Lahiff devised a plan to stop champion Burgers full forward Bob Pratt. It required courage on the part of Goss.

'Full back Lance "Diver" Dobson was to stick close to the dangerous Pratt, and rugged back-pocket player Norm Goss was to assist Dobson by blocking Pratt's path and stalling his spectacular leaps at every opportunity,' wrote Ken Linnett in his outstanding biography of Lahiff, *Game for Anything*. 'After the match Goss's back was a patchwork of stop marks from the boots of Bob Pratt, but he and Dobson had obeyed instructions with vigour and skill.'

Goss had stints at South Melbourne and Hawthorn, playing eight senior games for the Hawks in 1942 and 1943. He returned to Port Melbourne, was elected secretary in 1947 and held the position for three decades. He also gifted the club four senior players: Norm junior, Paul, Kevin and Michael. But he did not set out to make his sons Borough players. 'I just told them that if they were frightened they should become an umpire,' he once said.

Norm junior, Paul and Kevin played league football, with Norm winning a best and fairest at South Melbourne and figuring in Hawthorn's 1978 premiership.

Cook came to think of Norm Goss as his second father.

'Old Man Goss? Wonderful man, wonderful man,' he says. 'I'd nodded to him a couple of times, but I'd never met him before he asked me to play at Port. Soon saw what a great human being he was. He didn't drink, he didn't smoke, he was a good Catholic, he had about twenty-seven kids! He ruled that club very firmly — you couldn't push him back an inch, even with a bulldozer — and his word was everything. By geez, it was. I had a handshake deal with him. That was enough for me.'

Brice says Goss was not only a great administrator, but a fine spotter of talent. Careful not to pay more than the club could afford, for years he did most of the recruiting, assessing the needs of the team and finding players to strengthen it.

His mere presence on the interchange bench during matches was enough to motivate the Borough. 'He was respected so much that it was often about not just winning, but trying to do the right thing by Norm,' Brice says.

When Cook was entrenched at full forward, Goss would approach him before the game. If it was muddy and wet he would say Port would win if he could manage four goals. When conditions were better he would set a target of eight. Cook, never wanting to let him down, set his mind to it.

'That was his way of geeing me up, setting me a benchmark,' he says. 'If I did my job he might give me a nod of approval. He was a hard marker. If I kicked ten he might say, "You did okay today, pal."'

Norm Goss junior says his father thought highly of Cook, who was a regular visitor to the Goss home, often dropping in for a cup of tea and a chat before training.

'The old man and Fred were pretty close,' Goss junior says. 'Good mates, you could say. Fred was always himself around the old man.

He was a character, a huge personality. Confident.'

Norm Goss could be pleased with his prized recruit's first season at the North Port Oval.

Cook, playing mostly in the backline, had a season haul of 433 kicks (and only twenty-six handballs!) and 219 marks. He also kicked twenty-three goals, an appetiser for the feasts that followed. Four came against Prahran. After one, he was photographed raising both hands in triumph, a Two Blues defender dropping his head in disappointment. It became a familiar sight at VFL grounds.

Bonnett, now eighty-one, says he played Cook forward occasionally, and would have done more often but for his desire to 'be in the play all the time'.

'Because he was such a good mark, a wonderful mark in fact, he was always going to be dangerous in front of the goals,' he says.

But Bonnett, twelve times Port's leading goalkicker, could not have imagined that the player he laughingly remembers as a 'lazy bugger who loved the limelight' would surpass his tally of 933 goals. They were kicked, it must be pointed out, in more congested eighteen-a-side football and a low-scoring era.

When Port named its team of the century in 2003, Bonnett was in a forward pocket and Cook at full forward.

'Fred wasn't the best kick in the world, but he never went far from the goal square,' Bonnett says. 'There he could take his marks, and go back and put them straight through.'

That was all to come. A strong first season in Borough blue and red behind him, Cook looked forward to playing under Collins in the 1972 season. But a heart attack flattened him like no opponent could.

7

THE pain hit at half time. It was as if someone had taken a knife, plunged it into Fred Cook's chest and repeatedly twisted it.

'Something's not right here,' he remembers telling a teammate. 'Geez, I feel crook.'

Maybe it was just indigestion and it would pass, he thought.

Port Melbourne was playing Brunswick in a practice match and he had taken a heavy hit in the second quarter. But Cook played on, and by the end of the game had seventeen marks and four goals.

He showered, dressed and had a few beers in the social rooms, as he always did. But he remained unwell and decided to drive home. He never made it.

The pain in his chest became worse and, knowing the situation was serious, he headed for the Footscray home of the Port Melbourne club doctor, Evan Day.

Unable to get out of his car, he jabbed at the horn until Day appeared. The doctor quickly concluded Cook had suffered a heart attack. They made for the Footscray Hospital. Cook's family was called and was shocked to learn of his condition.

Football writer Alf Brown broke the news to *Herald* readers the next morning. 'Fred Cook, the VFA best and fairest two years ago, had a heart attack after starring in a practice match yesterday,' read his story under the headline 'Heart attack puts VFA star out'. The story said, 'He may not be able to play football again.'

Brown reported that Norm Goss had spoken to Fred Cook senior, who said doctors told him his son might have to retire from football.

'They banged a heap of morphine into me, a shitload, and when I came to I was thinking, *What in the stuff has happened here?*' Cook says. 'Through the glass I could see my mum looking at me and crying, and my old man and my brother and sisters were looking pretty upset. It was early doors. No-one knew exactly what was going on. But as for playing again, they were writing me off for all money. My wife was standing with a specialist at the end of my bed. He said, "Don't know that he'll play much football, but he might be able to have a swim with the kids."'

Surrounded by get-well cards, Cook spent three weeks in hospital and another six resting at home. Tests at The Alfred Hospital four months later showed his coronary arteries were clear.

In a show of support that Cook has never forgotten, Port Melbourne arranged a 'pleasant Sunday morning' on 7 May to raise money for him. 'All male supporters' were asked to attend.

What caused the heart attack? Cook says specialists formed the view that the knock he received during the game had dislodged a rib, pushing fatty tissue into his bloodstream. It blocked an artery. The chances of it happening were a million to one.

Cook was told his heart had undergone 'great trauma'. Rest wasn't recommended, it was necessary. He had to stop playing football.

Cook's response was blunt: he said he'd rather die.

In hindsight, he says, it was a foolish thing to say. They were the words of a brash young man with no concept of life and death. 'But it showed how much football meant to me,' he says. 'What you've got to understand is, it was the only thing I was good at, the only thing I did well in life. What was I going to do without football? I lived for it.'

Cook set himself to play again — as early as possible. After three months of taking it easy, he began to do some light training and gym work. The desire to get back burned inside him. Dr Day monitored him and encouraged him to quit smoking. More than forty years later, Cook is merrily puffing away.

Cook had thought the 1972 season would be his best and he wanted to salvage something of it, particularly if Port Melbourne could make a run at the finals.

'I am so keen to play again that it actually hurts to watch a football match,' he told reporter Phil Andrews. 'I shouldn't really go and watch Port on Sunday because it seems to make me feel low for the rest of the week. I want to get out there and join in.'

Adding to his frustration, the Borough had recruited two giants of the game — champion former South Melbourne rover Bob Skilton, and Melbourne and Carlton great Ron Barassi. Skilton won the best and fairest and finished third in the J. J. Liston Trophy, despite playing only eleven games. Barassi played three.

The league greats featured in Port Melbourne's Round 1 team against Sandringham, helping attract a crowd of 9000 people. The Borough went down by eight points. *Sun* reporter Stephen Phillips praised Skilton — '[he] started slowly, gathered momentum and finished strongly' — but said Barassi, then thirty-six, was disappointing. 'Barassi was not fast enough to the ball and when he did get there in time he was bundled out of the way.'

In his column in the *Sun*, Barassi said Zebra players had chipped him with comments like, 'You're too old, Grandpa,' and, 'Did you bring your wheelchair, Barass?' He said he wouldn't play on 'if I'm just going to be a struggling VFA player'. Barassi was gone after two more matches.

Collins, meanwhile, was missing his mobile big man Cook. He remembers that Port lacked goal-to-goal line height in 1972, and he could have done with Cook in defence and in the ruck. 'He would have made an enormous difference. He was a very good player,' Collins says.

Cook approached Norm Goss about a comeback, but the secretary sternly shook his head and said it was out of the question. Too early, he said. Too risky. 'Then clear me to another club,' Cook shot back. 'I'm ready to play.'

Finally, he had his way. Port Melbourne tried to take out an insurance policy on him — 'I suppose they thought I'd sue them if I dropped dead in a game,' Cook quips — but failed. He was, however, selected in the seconds team to play Oakleigh on Saturday 19 August.

And he made a spectacular re-entry, kicking sixteen goals in a 120-point victory. *Sun* man Phillips called it 'probably one of the greatest comebacks ever'.

Up until then, Cook thought the full forward position was for 'pansies', taking the glory for the grunt work of players up the ground. But he was named there to reduce the risk of heavy knocks.

'I think I had thirty shots at goals. Flogged 'em,' Cook says of his return game. He was promoted to the senior team for the last match of the season, against Coburg, and he kicked five goals (Peter Smith, the son of legendary league coach Norm, made way for him despite having kicked seventy-seven).

He looked in good shape. Before the Coburg match, *Age* scribe Geoffrey Frithall noted Cook 'trained hard and looked one of the fittest members of the squad'. Dr Day had seen to that, joining his patient on runs. Cook felt reassured that help would be at hand if he took ill again.

But there were mental demons to conquer. Cook says it was always in the back of his mind that he may have another heart attack, despite having gained a medical clearance. When he got a touch of cramp, he wondered if it was the onset of something more serious.

Port Melbourne player and *Herald* reporter Julian Swinstead worried, too. Most of Cook's teammates, he wrote, thought it was wrong for him to play football and risk his health. 'It is a strange feeling to play alongside a footballer who you know could have a serious attack at any moment. On long pre-season training runs, as the sweat is pouring from everyone, you wonder whether Fred will make it or not. He's normally first home.'

The match against Coburg was Cook's sole senior appearance in 1972 — the Borough finished fifth, a game outside the four. But he'd found himself a new position. Where he had been a defender, now he was a full forward.

ı|ı|ı

IN 2008, the VFL, keen to woo a bigger crowd to its season showpiece, decided to stage a night grand final at Etihad Stadium. It was set down for the eve of the AFL decider.

Ian Collins was running Etihad, and in a nod to the history of the VFA, stadium and league officials came up with the idea of naming the ends after two great goalkickers — Fred Cook of Port Melbourne and Jim 'Frosty' Miller of Dandenong.

Collins had played with both men (Cook at Port, Miller at Carlton) and they were asked to appear at the ground for a photo shoot. Collins playfully held them apart. The joke went that no-one wanted to see another outbreak of hostilities to match the violent 1976 grand final.

When Collins saw Cook that day, he reminded him that he was the coach who first played him at full forward. 'I made you, Fred!' Cook remembers his old mentor quipping.

'That's quite true,' Collins says now. 'I did tell him I could take some credit for him kicking all those goals! He'd had that heart attack after the practice match and I had a real concern that if we played him and he died on the footy field, we'd have been liable for his demise. We sought to get an insurance policy to protect ourselves, but we couldn't get it. So, I didn't want him running around too much. We played him full forward in the reserves, he kicked many goals just standing in the goal square and from then on that was his position. He went from strength to strength.'

That was no surprise, Collins says, noting that Cook was 'big and strong and had good judgement and was hard to knock off balance'.

Collins chuckles as he recalls how Cook, never the hardest trainer, would approach him at training in 1973 and complain of chest pains. 'So I'd say, "Go on Fred, have a shower and go home." Knowing him, he was probably going out somewhere that night!'

But he flourished in front of the goals, kicking sixty-seven goals in 1973 and settling fifth on the league table. Miller topped it with 108. Sandringham's Ian Cooper, with 104, also ticked into triple figures. Geelong West's Graeme McLean went agonisingly close, with ninety-nine.

Four of Cook's goals came in a match against Prahran. He remembers it with a curse: Collins started him on the bench.

'Can you believe it? He put me on the bench. I said to Collo after the game, "Don't be doing that again." But go and look up the result. I came on and turned the bloody game. Proved a point.'

Indeed he did. Introduced after half time, he got busy as Port won by seventeen points. 'Proved your mettle today,' Norm Goss told him after the match.

Collins has no memory of spelling his star, but says he would have been trying to sting him into action. Cook, he says, could be a little wayward and needed a firm word now and then. 'Larger than life, Fred. Always on the edge. But one of those blokes who wouldn't do you a bad turn. Likeable, friendly.'

With a new and exciting spearhead, Port Melbourne finished the home-and-away season with eleven wins and seven losses, good enough for third. But it lost to Prahran in the first semi.

That year, *Herald* readers learned more about Cook in a memorable full-page article written by Claudia Wright. She related a scene in which he emerged from the showers to dry his hair with an electric brush, and slap on aftershave and underarm deodorant. Tommy Lahiff was watching and said with disgust, 'All these young blokes … in my day we didn't have hot showers … had cold ones and dried ourselves with a bit of hessian — have a look at this poofter.'

Wright called Cook 'touchy, headstrong, generous and has a tremendous male chauvinist background'.

'He has been programmed 100 percent male,' Wright said. 'He knows little about women. He keeps talking about going home to the dragon and the goblins … "the missus and the billy lids".'

By that stage the Cooks had three children: Jacqueline, Tracie and Nathan. Yet in conversation with Wright, he spoke about 'being with girls … that air of excitement … what's going to happen when you're together'.

Cook says Bernadette was displeased with his comments. 'I wasn't thrilled with the whole thing either,' Cook says. 'Made me look a bit stupid. Twisted things around.' But he agreed with Wright's description of his wife. She called her 'tolerant'.

ı|lı

CHEST pains came back to Fred Cook on the night of 22 September 1974. Feeling a thump, thump, thump, he thought he had better take himself off to hospital. Doctors at The Alfred assessed him and said he was dehydrated, but otherwise fine.

No doubt he was feeling giddy from all the champagne he'd been guzzling. It was premiership bubbly — hours earlier, Port Melbourne had defeated Oakleigh by sixty-nine points in the grand final at the Junction Oval.

And Cook had played a starring role. For the first time in his career, he kicked ten goals (he did it on twenty-one more occasions), putting up the biggest bag in a season-decider since Borough champion Ted Freyer's twelve in 1940.

Jim Buckley was among the best on the ground with almost forty disposals and set the seal on an outstanding season by winning his second best and fairest.

The victory made for a first-up flag for new coach Norm Brown, the three-time Fitzroy best and fairest big man who had replaced Collins.

To the team that had narrowly missed the finals, the Borough added class players Darryl Herrod (ex-Geelong and Fitzroy), Ian Owen (Richmond) and Mick Erwin (Collingwood and Richmond), and teased improvement out of local lads David 'Sam' Holt, Graeme Anderson, Paul Goss and Graham 'Buster' Harland. Port was minor premier with fifteen wins and three losses, and added two finals victories to claim its tenth premiership.

Cook's only blemish in the grand final came late in the last quarter, when the ball was kicked into the forward line and hit him in the neck.

He wasn't watching the play. His mind was elsewhere. Before the match Cook and four other people, including Ted Whitten, had pooled their money and put $3000 on Port to win the flag. Near the end of the game, Cook spied the Oakleigh supporter with whom he had laid the bet, watching him walk through the crowd and towards the gate. But before he left, the Oakleigh barracker sought out Norm Goss and handed over a brown paper bag solid with money. Goss gave it to Cook after the game.

Later, when all the champagne tipped into an empty stomach made him feel ill, he took the bag with him to hospital, placing it in his underpants. A nurse noticed the bulge. Cook quickly had to explain what he was hiding.

Whitten popped in soon after. 'How are you feeling?' he asked. When Cook said he was fine, Whitten shot back: 'Great. Now, did you get paid?'

Fred Cook senior, who was also in on the bet, came by. 'Get the money?' was the first thing he said. Relieved the winnings had been collected, he asked his son how he was doing. 'The old man had his priorities right,' Cook says with a guffaw.

Betting on VFA games was common back then, Cook says, recalling the day when two bookmakers approached him before a game against Williamstown. They asked him to feign an ankle injury and limp off the ground. In return they would give him $2000.

Cook thought about it for thirty seconds. He figured that by going off with an injury he wouldn't lose face with teammates or officials. And he would pocket a handsome sum. 'But I said I couldn't do it,' he says. 'Couldn't let down the club like that. What if Old Man Goss heard about it? When they knew I wasn't going to take a dive, the bookies went and backed Port. They made a bit. I kicked a few and we won the game.'

Cook relished playing under Brown, thinking him a hard but fair coach and a player who never took a backward step. The players liked him.

'Was he a good coach?' Cook says. 'Well, he got the results and that's always the best way to judge 'em. He knew how to get the best out of you.'

He remembers a match when Port was struggling and Brown gave his players a gee-up at three-quarter time. As Cook and Holt were walking away from the huddle, he rounded them up and roared, 'Get out there and do something, will you!'

'I think Sam kicked a couple and I kicked a couple, and we won the game,' Cook says. 'That's all he had to say to us. We were playing like old women and he put the wind up us.'

Cook says it would have been a travesty if Port Melbourne failed to win the 1974 premiership. It had a 'dream team' and it was his privilege to be on the end of 'lace-up' passes from future Collingwood half forward Anderson and Holt. '"Browny" had an embarrassment of riches, really,' Cook says.

He says a typical passage of play involved Brown or Brendan Behan winning a tap in the ruck at half back, presenting possession to Paul Goss or Jim Buckley. They in turn would find Anderson or Harland, who would sweep through the centre and drill a pass to Cook. 'The full back didn't stand a chance, the poor bugger,' Cook says. 'We were a bit like a machine, really.'

His cog turned for sixty-eight goals, second on the VFA table to Dandenong great Miller, whose seventy-nine goals had him topping the competition charts for the sixth time.

Cook found that the more he set goal umpires' flags waving, the greater the expectations of him. He would be more relieved than pleased when he walked off with a bag. Echoing the words of many other sportspeople, he says it was easier to reach the top than stay there.

'You kick a few and everyone expects you to kick a few more. It creates a lot of bloody pressure. By playing well, you set a mark for yourself and that's what you've got to reach each and every game. If you don't, you're seen as a failure in a lot of people's eyes,' Cook says. 'I remember a selection meeting when I was vice-captain and a selector. We were going through the side to play Mordialloc and we were talking about picking guys on form. And, not a word of a lie, Old Man Goss turned around, looked me in the eye and said, "On your last half of football you should be dropped." Cheeky bugger. He played me like a fiddle.'

Cook couldn't bear the thought of letting down the small army of Borough anklebiters which turned up for every game in No. 5 jumpers and changed ends every quarter to help wave through his goals. He wanted to send them home smiling and have them talking about 'Fabulous Fred' at school on Mondays.

Cook liked to start well, feeding his confidence. He knew he was having a day out when he lost count of how many he had kicked.

Years later, when his career was winding down and the goals were drying up, he would pull aside teammates as they were taking their positions and ask them to look out for him.

Jason Love, who made a dazzling entrance to Port's senior team in 1984, recalls, 'Freddie would always say to me, "Young fella, young fella, make sure you look after me early, I need to get on the board." He wanted the old Joe Goose over the top as soon as the game started.'

Love laughs and adds: 'He wouldn't give one back though, I can assure you of that!'

8

IT became a common sight in the VFA and it never failed to quicken the pulses of Port Melbourne supporters. The ball entered to the forward line and Fred Cook, tall and strong, raised his Frisbee-sized hands, marked and kicked a goal, setting blue and red flags fluttering.

Years later, as they sit in the Norm Goss grandstand, long-tooth Borough watchers go tender at the memory. It was a long time ago, but they have never forgotten the spectacle of the big man ruling the goal square.

They saw him do it for sixty-seven goals in 1973, and sixty-eight in 1974. But his game ascended to a higher level in 1975 and an aura began to surround him.

'You never wanted to take your eyes off him, because he always made something happen,' Bob Doughty, sixty, and a 55-year Borough barracker, says. 'He was just so great to watch.'

Doughty liked to watch from the now-demolished small grandstand behind the goals. With an elevated view a short distance from the fence, he could see everything.

Cook's season started with seven goals against Dandenong, and he reached his first century in the final home-and-away round against Geelong West. A crowd of 8000 was at North Port Oval to watch him achieve what Rooster Joe Radojevic did the previous week.

Led by David Holt's six goals, Port had a 36-point advantage at the final siren. But the Roosters finished with one more win and the minor premiership.

Two weeks after Cook topped the ton, the clubs met in the second semi-final, and Geelong West won by twenty-two points. It put Port up against its great rival Dandenong.

In a classic preliminary final, the Redlegs came from behind to triumph by four points. Cook booted six goals. 'We played in mud and shit at the Junction,' he says. 'That buggered us up because we were a skilled side. But it was disappointing to lose both those finals. We weren't used to it at Port Melbourne.' He avoided Norm Goss after the match.

Cook could find consolation with a season haul of 108 goals, second on the list behind Radojevic (119), who kicked four in the grand final as his club won its first First Division title.

Knowing the attention they received from defenders, Cook had great admiration for Radojevic, Miller and Prahran's Kim Smith. All were supreme spearheads. Miller booted 883 goals, Radojevic 723 and Smith 610.

'If you were a full forward back then, you always knew you'd be in for a hard day,' Cook says. 'If you went for a mark, nine times out of ten you'd cop a smack in the back of the head. It was a hell of a lot easier to punch someone in the head than punch a ball coming down at 100 miles an hour. Harold Martin [Preston great] played on me one day. My head was shaped like a bloody pumpkin at the end of the game.'

Radojevic laughs how he remembers that defenders relished a 'follow through' with their fists in their spoiling attempts. With only one field umpire, there were few free kicks to be had for forwards. Radojevic was more surprised when a clip didn't arrive than when it did. 'You expected it,' he says. 'That's just how it was.'

But his teammates say Cook steadfastly stayed in front and absorbed the bumps without complaint. They all acknowledge his wonderful marking. But they also marvel at his courage. No one can recall him flinching in the face of opposition fire.

'He had a lot of heart, Freddie,' Norm Goss junior says. 'Very gutsy. Fearless.'

Norm Brown says Cook had eyes only for the ball, when some opponents had eyes only for him. 'He never shirked an issue. No worries there. He wasn't an aggressive type, he didn't belt blokes; he just went for the ball very strongly. He copped some beauties, but always got up and went on with the game.'

Gary Brice saw it, too. He says Cook 'copped some unbelievable whacks' and 'took a battering'. Brice adds, 'But he had tremendous courage. Even though he was a big bloke, to play in front all the time the way he did was amazing.'

Cook prided himself on being deaf to the sound of what he calls 'the thundering hooves'. He would not be intimidated. If there was a mark in the offering, he would go for it regardless of his position. If it meant running back with the flight of the ball, so be it. If he got hurt, he did his best to hide it. He never wanted to give defenders the satisfaction of seeing him in pain.

'I got back at them in another way,' he says. 'If a bloke gave me a clip on the chin and opened me up, it might take ten days to heal. But if I kicked a shitload of goals on him, that was going to stay with him forever. Would be a permanent scar. He'd always think, *That bastard stitched me up good and proper, made me look like a dill*.'

Cook feared only one opponent — Coburg's Trevor Price. He thought Price a decent player, but 'plain crazy'. Cook says, 'I was shit-frightened of him. My word, I was. Hated it when I saw him coming down the forward line to pick me up. The night before we played them I used to sleep with the lights on.'

And when Port played intra-club practice matches he was wary of Bob 'Bullwinkle' Profitt, despite them being premiership teammates. 'He was wild,' Cook says. 'I'd try to keep him sweet. Same with Trevor Price. I'd say, "Not your fault I kicked that one, it's those bloody half backs, they won't pick up their men. You're going okay."'

Profitt treated practice games as he did home-and-away matches, giving no favours and expecting none. 'I always used to think that if you took it easy, the bloke at the other end was going to get your spot in the side,' he says.

Before the 1976 grand final, Port coach Norm Brown told his players they'd be having a short scratch match. 'Don't put that fucking idiot on me,' Cook roared. Profitt looked around. 'Who's he talking about?' he asked. It can only be you, Bullwinkle, his teammates replied. Profitt got his own back, breaking Cook's nose in a marking contest. 'I went to punch the ball and got Fred instead,' he says.

Cook rarely got involved in fighting, preferring to strike his blows on the scoreboard. He would occasionally enter a melee and throw his weight around, but it was more about being seen to support teammates than deal with opponents. They rarely needed help, anyway. The only time he can recall retaliating to rough treatment was when a Preston opponent kicked him in the calf as he set out on a lead. Cook turned and delivered a classic 'coathanger' to the Bullant. It sparked an all-players-in stoush, at the end of which Cook was given a free kick. The umpire didn't see the incident, but told him, 'I knew something must have happened for you to react like that, Fred.'

In the many games he watched Port Melbourne, VFA writer Marc Fiddian saw Cook swing punches only once, in a match against

Sandringham. It was so out of character, he wrote, that pressmen quizzed Port officials about it after the game. They said he had a broken hand and was sick of having it grabbed.

Cook had a lot of hard men around him. He remembers the day a young Graeme Anderson was being accosted by a Preston opponent. Bizarrely, the Bullant was grabbing at the Port player's groin. Cook informed Mick Erwin, and instructed Anderson to run his opponent through centre half forward. Erwin was waiting. The Preston player's day was over. 'Gave him a coathanger,' Erwin recalls with a laugh. 'But the guy had it coming. He'd been harassing Arms [Anderson] for ten minutes. He came my way. The rest is history. I didn't do stuff like that often, but we'd had enough.'

Wherever Cook looked he saw Boroughs who were good to be around when there was clear and present danger — Profitt, the Goss brothers, George Allen, Greg Dermott, 'Buster' Harland.

Any player who roughed him up also felt the wrath of Port supporters, as Martin found. Martin was one of the leading VFA ruckmen in the 1970s, but occasionally played on Cook to cancel out the height advantage he had over most full backs. Martin admits he dealt with him 'rather unfairly' a few times, but Cook never responded. Port barrackers, however, were outraged. 'Fred was their hero and they wanted to kill you any time you touched him,' he says. 'I was lucky to get off the ground there one day. You took your life into your own hands.'

Later, Martin was non-playing coach of Coburg. In a match at Port Melbourne in 1982, he grew increasingly frustrated as Cook received what he thought were 'soft' free kicks.

At half time he approached Cook and asked, 'Are you rooting the umpire, Fred?' Cook responded by playfully cuddling the whistleblower. Martin also approached the umpire, tapping him on the back of the head. The Port Melbourne supporters were incensed. 'Because I've upstaged Freddie, the crowd have gone absolutely mad,' Martin recalls. 'When I went to the rooms they were punching the wire on the players' race and abusing me like you wouldn't believe. There must have been 10,000 people there and they all wanted a piece of me. It was an interesting old day, that one.'

ı|ı

FRED Cook played 300 games in the VFA and dominated many of them. But if there's one match for which he's most remembered, it's the 1976 grand final between Port and Dandenong.

The old association was known for its 'biffo' — indeed, it was part of its attraction — but the decider at the Junction Oval was at another, uglier level.

Nine players and officials were reported, but if it had been scrutinised as microscopically as today's AFL games, with repeated video viewings, the tribunal might have sat for a month. Marc Fiddian called the second term of the grand final 'possibly the most vicious quarter of football in VFA history'.

Cook was at the heart of it. Five minutes into the term, he was flattened behind play by Dandenong defender Allan Harper, setting off wild scenes. Moments earlier, he'd intercepted a kick from teammate Billy Swan and casually popped it through the goals, his third for the match.

Port's anger at the treatment of its full forward can be judged by a photograph published in *The Age* the day after the match. Cook is facedown on the ground, legs splayed. Harper stands over him. And in the foreground Borough coach Norm Brown runs towards them, his mouth agape and his right fist clenched.

Brown was seeing red. He was the first to arrive, flailing at Harper, who spun to stand his ground. Port youngster Calvin Kerr came in at speed, meeting Harper heavily. They fell to the ground to wrestle. Soon a circle of fighting players surrounded them, four umpires doing their best to separate them. At the other end of the ground, Port's George Allen dealt with champion Dandenong forward Pat Flaherty. The commotion bubbled away for five minutes.

After trainers and Port doctor Lynne Maddern helped Cook to his feet, he raised his arms to signal he was okay. 'Nah, I wasn't okay,' he says. 'I thought I was at a hockey match. Was away with the fairies. Didn't know where the fuck I was. But I knew I had to get up. What do they say? Champions get up when they can't.'

Later in the quarter, Harper decked the burly Brown with a left hook as he ran towards the boundary line, dislodging teeth. Buster Harland was so close he heard the thwack of fist on face. Incensed, he responded by putting Harper to the ground. 'It was time to even things up,' Harland recalls. 'It was a sickening hit on Fred.'

More fisticuffs followed.

'This is shades of sixty-seven!' commentator Phil Gibbs declared, referring to the controversial 1967 grand final between the same clubs at the Punt Road ground.

Harper escaped report, but he did not escape retribution: the blow from Harland broke his jaw and he didn't play after half time. He spent grand final night at The Alfred Hospital.

The newspapers gave the match big treatment.

'Umpire felled in brawl' screamed page 1 of *The Sun*, reporting that boundary umpire Colin Walker had put Port big man Tony Haenen in the book for assaulting him (he was cleared at the tribunal).

The headlines 'Violent Sunday' and 'VFA final bloodbath' ran across the back page. The two main photographs featured Cook, one of him motionless on the ground and the other back on his feet, with blood pouring from his mouth.

'I reckon it was the first and only time the VFA was on the front and back pages of the *Sun* on a Monday morning,' Flaherty says. 'Don't forget, the league preliminary final was on that weekend. It was big news. It was pretty wild, wasn't it?'

In *The Age*, Fiddian said players had 'resorted to violence in what was proving a shocking advertisement for the VFA.' He quoted Port Melbourne officials as saying 'the attack on Cook was the most cowardly we've seen.'

Phil Cleary wrote in *Cleary Independent* that Harper 'went berserk, king hitting unsuspecting Port full forward Fred Cook, then repeating the dose on captain-coach Norm Brown.' He added, 'For twenty minutes the estimated crowd of 30,000 and a massive television audience watched in disbelief as violation and retribution usurped a game of football.'

'Jesus Christ, am I glad I'm not out there,' Cleary had thought.

At half time, and without anaesthetic, Maddern stitched Cook, who was cut inside and out. Fred Cook senior held one of his arms and head trainer Bertie Wilsmore the other. A concerned Norm Goss stood close by. Thinking his day was done, Cook asked Goss who would play full forward in the second half. 'What's wrong with you? You don't run on your fucking chin!' Goss shot back. It dissolved tension in the rooms; people who heard it walked away chuckling.

After the grand final, Cook was told that Harper said before the match he would knock Cook out if he started getting on top. But he carries no grudges towards 'Big Al'. 'Shit like that happened in those days,' Cook says. 'Some brutal stuff went on. I played reasonably well and we won the premiership, which is what we were there to do.'

Flaherty confirms Harper had it in his mind to stop Cook by whatever means necessary. 'On the Thursday night ... I don't know whether I should be saying this but ... after training I was having a shower with Allan Harper and he said, "I'm not going to be made to look a fool of." He said if Cook kicked three goals he was going to cop one. And that's as true as I stand here. So I think he always had it in his mind that he was going to do something stupid. Well, people say things before games and it doesn't always happen, does it?'

Harper, sixty, prefers not to talk about what he refers to as 'the incidents' with Cook and Brown. He says it's all been 'well documented' and it's 'pointless going over it'.

As for Brown, he never saw the blow coming. He gets tired of seeing footage of it when he returns to Port for reunions, regarding it as 'water under the bridge'. Referring to Harper's pre-game pledge, Brown says with a laugh, 'Well, he pulled the trigger early!'

Harland — who as a boy was strong enough to lift steel grates out of footpaths, earning the nickname 'Buster' after *Tarzan the Fearless* actor Buster Crabbe — received a six-match suspension for striking Harper. He has no regrets. 'I did what I had to do,' he says. 'It was all part and parcel of it. When I was younger I actually thought it was a bit of fun. Didn't bother me much.'

At the instigation of Dandenong president Geoff Tucker, some of the Dandy and Port Melbourne players met a few days after the grand final to smooth things over. Harper and Cook had a game of billiards and he apologised to the spearhead.

'I am actually sorry about a few other incidents,' Harper, who played nine senior games for St Kilda in 1973 and 1974, says.

'You can't take it back. I'm just thankful I didn't do any long-lasting damage to anybody. The game was a different game in those days. As I say, I can't take it back, but obviously I regret it. I'd played on Fred before. He had some great days on me and I had some good days on him. It was a bit of a mismatch on weight and height, but anyway, someone had to play on him.'

Just as Cook has no ill feeling towards Harper, Flaherty does not resent Allen's action. He says the Port defender actually apologised before decking him. 'Harper hit Cook and George saw it. He was standing just behind me on the right-hand side, and he yelled out something and he said, "I'm sorry for this," and went *whack!* I remember it like it was yesterday. Knocked the stuffing out of me. Anyway, I did play the game out. But I have no problem with George whatsoever. I've seen George plenty of times. We've had a beer. He's a good bloke. As far as I was concerned, what happened on the field stayed out there.'

Harper thought Dandenong had an excellent team and was confident it could win the grand final. But he and Flaherty remember that the wind, a 'howling gale', changed at quarter time and the Redlegs kicked into it for the first half.

'It was only in the third quarter that we had use of it. But no-one ever remembers that. They just think we got flogged,' Flaherty says. 'But we didn't have much luck. They would have still probably beaten us — they were a damn great side.'

Port, taking a streak of eleven wins into the match, romped it in by fifty-seven points. Cook kicked four goals and was named among the best, alongside Harland, Allen, Haenen and Shane Molloy.

Cook remembers the Borough of 1976 as an outstanding team, with fine players on every line: Bob Profitt, Greg Dermott, Allen,

Shane Molloy, Ian Owen and Paul Wharton in defence; future champion Billy Swan in the middle; Ivan Rasmussen and David Holt across half forward; Haenen and Brown in the ruck; and Jim Christou and Harland on the ball.

Alloyed to their skills was a fitness base that gave them the confidence they could finish games as well as they started them. After a shocking mid-season loss to Coburg, Brown and Norm Goss called in league boundary umpire and notable runner Peter Saultry as the fitness man.

'They're not fit,' Saultry said when they bailed him up in the rooms after the game. 'They've been having fundraising for their end-of-season trip. They've gone backwards.'

Saultry, who had done a ten-week stint with Port before the season, took no nonsense. He had a job to do and went about it with a drill sergeant's zeal (he later served the club as president from 1992 to 2011, steering it to financial security).

'I was always a great believer in having a solid foundation,' Saultry says. 'You can't get away from it. It's not easy, it's not enjoyable, but in the end it's very beneficial. Don't let anyone tell you Port was lucky to win premierships. The players worked their arses off.'

Cook didn't care for the running, but came to appreciate its value. 'He [Saultry] took us to another level. He put us in better physical condition than anyone else.'

One hot night, Saultry had the players run from the North Port Oval to the Shrine of Remembrance, there to do sprint work. They then had to get back to North Port. As they started their journey, Cook and a few teammates noticed a tradesman stuck in traffic on St Kilda Road. They jumped in the back of his ute and hitched a ride to the ground.

'Trouble was, they bobbed their heads up on Normanby Road, so I caught them,' Saultry says. 'They got their penalties, don't worry about that.'

Cook had been held goalless by Coburg's Ron Beattie during the season. But in the return game he kicked ten, telling Phil Cleary at quarter time: 'No-one keeps me goalless twice in a season.' He'd earlier told umpire Frank Vergona, 'It won't fucking happen again, Frankie.'

He finished the 1976 season with the club best and fairest, his tallest total in a match (fourteen against Sandringham to nullify Bob Murray's ten for the Zebras) and an aggregate of 124 goals, topping the VFA list for the first time. He was only getting started. There were more centuries and premierships to come.

ı|||ı

AS he watched Fred Cook pile up the goals for Port Melbourne, North Melbourne secretary Ron Joseph got thinking: this guy's too good for the VFA. Joseph was a canny judge of football talent, and believed Cook could hold his own in the league and be a useful player for the Kangaroos.

After all, he'd played thirty-odd games for the Bulldogs and did reasonably well. So Joseph picked up the phone and arranged to meet the Borough pin-up boy. Cook has since told a lot of people that, if it had worked out, he would have been the full forward in North Melbourne's 1977 premiership team.

'Yes, I did have a crack at Freddie,' Joseph says. 'He'd had a really good year with Port — in fact he'd had two or three really top seasons — and by that stage Wadey [the great goalkicker Doug Wade] had left us. I can't really remember if Fred came down and trained. But I've got a feeling he did, you know.'

Cook says he did have a couple of Sunday morning training sessions with the Roos at Kensington, and he slipped in for a North pre-season intraclub match, having the better of Ross Glendinning. He recalls Ray 'Slug' Jordon sledging him before the game, saying, in typically colourful terms, that he was about to find out what real football was all about.

Glendinning says he did line up on Cook, but in a scratch match against Port Melbourne at the North Port Oval before the 1977 season. He recalls the hit-out for the fact that Robbie Briedis had a couple of 'stand-ups' with Port players (Briedis's brother, North Melbourne forward Arnold, later joined the Borough) and that his North teammate Roy Ramsay was Port star Billy Swan's cousin.

Glendinning cannot recall how many goals he conceded. 'He did kick some, definitely. I'd be reluctant to say exactly how many, but he did kick some. Whether it was three, four or five, I don't know.'

Joseph has no doubt Cook would have made a good fist of a second league chance, particularly under the coaching of Ron Barassi. Barassi, he points out, rarely failed to get the best out of a player.

'They probably would have had their fall-outs, but not too many people who played under 'Barass' played below their ability. Fred Cook wouldn't have been any different. Had things gone the right way for him at the outset, with a bloke like Barassi as his coach, I reckon he could have been anything. There was a guy a bit like Freddie up in Albury. Stan Sargeant was his name and I always rated Stan Sargeant as the Doug Wade of country football. Freddie was certainly the Doug Wade of the VFA.'

Cook says the approach from North Melbourne initially excited him. The thought of players like Wayne Schimmelbusch, Keith Greig and Barry Cable kicking the ball to him made him catch his breath.

He figured he only had to take four marks a game, or one a quarter, to get four goals. 'If you kick four goals in twenty-two matches, suddenly you've got close to 100. I really believed in my heart I could do it,' he says. 'I could mark the ball. I never heard thundering hooves. I was an okay kick. I'd already stitched up the best full back in the land [Glendinning] when I was still drunk from the night before. Didn't have any sleep. Kicked six goals and missed two from the square.'

He says he had sleepless nights about leaving Port. Cook had become the most followed player in the VFA. Doors opened for him. His success in the association meant he cast a large shadow on football-mad Melbourne. What if he went to North and it didn't work out? Would people mark him down as a player? Would his standing in the VFA be the same? And wouldn't he disappoint the kids who wore his number on their Port Melbourne jumpers?

In the end, he says, the decision was out of his hands. 'I was still tied to Footscray and they wanted to make it hard for North. I got a letter from Ronnie Joseph saying it would be cheaper for North to pursue Peter Hudson than me because Footscray put such a high price tag on my head. He wished me good luck for the year at Port Melbourne. I was pretty relieved in the end. I didn't have to tell Old Man Goss I was pissing off.'

Joseph has no recall of the letter or any negotiations with the Bulldogs. But he says Cook's story sounds plausible. 'There was no love lost between North and most of the other clubs because we tried to raid any player we thought could win us a flag,' Joseph says. 'So it is possible they [Footscray] tried to stop it.'

Three years after Joseph raised the idea of getting Cook to the Kangaroos, ex-Magpie and Tiger Mick Erwin applied for the Footscray coaching job. He got down to the last two, eventually missing out to former Richmond champion Royce Hart.

If he had landed the position, Erwin would have tried to take Cook back to the Bulldogs — despite him being past the age of thirty. Erwin had played with Cook at Port in 1974 and 1975, and was convinced that, even as he nudged veteran status, he could be good for Footscray.

As he went through the interview process, Erwin spoke to Cook about a belated comeback. 'We had it down that he was going to return to Footscray if I was coach,' he says. 'Whether it would have been a success, we'll never know. But that's how highly I thought of him at that time.'

Erwin had assessed Footscray's forward division and concluded Cook would be a good acquisition, despite his advancing years. 'Age didn't matter, for what I wanted him to do, play full forward. They [the Bulldogs] had nothing like him. At that stage there wasn't all the fitness attached to the game. You used to have to get the ball down there quickly, none of this flicking it around like they do now. He would have been a great go-to man in the square, especially on the heavy grounds, when the pace went out of the game and it became slow and a bit of a slog. Freddie was a great mark in the wet. He was a great mark, full-stop.'

Erwin had always remembered a match he played in at Port when it came from behind to nose out Prahran at Toorak Park. Late in the final quarter, Cook outmarked four opponents 'who were trying to punch his head off'. Erwin asserts that in all his years of football he never saw a stronger mark. 'Fred hardly got off the ground. He just stood there and they crashed into him from all angles and he didn't flinch. He took the mark. He went back, kicked the goal, the ball went back to the centre and the siren went. It won us the game.

Unbelieavable. Same with his judgement and his discipline on the ground. They whacked him, they did everything to him, and Freddie never did anything but go for the ball. That's real courage. He was tough, mate. Most full forwards sleep with the lights on, but not Freddie. He was incredibly tough.'

Erwin suspects Cook's reputation as a poor trainer but a champion socialiser deterred league clubs from recruiting him.

Cook admits he was no great 'track worker' — football writer Alf Brown called him a 'bad trackhorse' who was reluctant to 'get out of the slow walk that he calls running'. But he says he never left a training session until he'd made quick leads and taken ten consecutive marks. It gave him confidence that his game was in order. His other routine came a few minutes before matches, when he would get a ball, throw it against a brick wall at all angles and catch the rebound, sharpening his reflexes and enjoying the feel of leather in his hands.

ı|ı

THE 1977 season heralded the centenary of the VFA — and Port Melbourne and Fred Cook made the occasion their own.

The Borough won the Centenary Cup (a knock-out competition) and the premiership, thrashing Sandringham to claim its third flag in four seasons. Quirkily, the winning margin in the hundredth year of the VFA was 100 points, a talking point when more than 1000 people gathered for the grand final celebration at the Royal Ballroom. The following day, players headed to coach Norm Brown's Southern Cross Hotel.

The courtship with North Melbourne behind him, Cook powered on with what had caught Joseph's discerning eye: his prodigious goalkicking.

He fired off 167 goals, including thirty in Centenary Cup fixtures and twelve in representative games. With Brown out with a knee injury, he captained Port in the grand final and his contribution was 9.4. Cook's returns in home-and-away games were 10, 6, 7, 3, 8, 5, 7, 10, 5, 3, 4, 8, 5, 7, 4, 5, 3 and 7, adding nine in both of his finals.

For all his brilliance, he failed to poll a vote in the J. J. Liston Trophy, despite the goal umpires allotting votes alongside the central umpire. 'Hard markers, umpires,' Cook says. *Herald* writer John Craven said it 'seems scandalous' the Port forward went unrecognised (at least he gained ten votes in the club best and fairest).

In Centenary Cup games, Cook booted six goals against Werribee, Coburg and Prahran, and twelve against Caulfield, and in National Football league matches he had five goals against Queensland and seven against Norwood. He also captained the VFA team against Queensland in Brisbane and nailed nine in a losing effort.

Picking his team of the year in *The Sporting Globe*, writer Michael Lovett installed Cook at full forward. 'I'm sure no-one would argue,' he wrote.

Port had a formidable side. The return of ruck star Vic Aanensen from South Melbourne and Paul Goss from Melbourne, the recruitment of former Collingwood star John Greening, Barry Beecroft (South Melbourne) and Peter Ivanoff (St Kilda), and the emergence of young Bernie Evans, had strengthened an already powerful line-up.

'I would say they are the best team I've seen in my time in VFA football,' Sandringham coach Darrell Mackenzie told *Sun* scribe Bill Hawker after the grand final.

But, emphasising the gulf between league and association teams, Port Melbourne secretary Jack 'Darky' McFarlane insisted the

Borough would get 'killed' by any VFL team.

The premiership team also contained two sons of Norm Goss, Paul and Kevin, who would go on to play twenty-four games for South Melbourne.

Brown says local products such as the Goss brothers, Harland, Dermott and Swan formed the foundation of his teams, and the club was 'topped up' with recruits. 'We just didn't go out and get whoever was around,' he says. 'If a league player became available, other clubs would buy him irrespective of where he played. If he was, say, a centreman, they'd buy him even if they already had a good centreman. We liked to pick and choose, and that was partly because we weren't the richest club in the association. You had to buy wisely. You didn't go and grab someone just for the sake of it. But we had a solid base, and that was the Port boys who'd come up through the seconds and thirds, and they were keen to do well and they looked after themselves.'

That meant few of his players went out socialising on Saturday nights. Brown said from the start that he didn't want to be fishing around the local pubs the night before matches, checking up on who was having a beer. He knew which of his players were drinkers and factored it into their performances. 'They knew if their form was bad and they got dropped they shouldn't come to me crying about it,' he says.

Brown had also increased Port's training load. There was ball work on Tuesdays and Thursdays, Saultry's running program on Wednesdays and, depending on the opposition the next day, a light run on Saturday morning.

He believes Port Melbourne was the first club to do three major sessions. Envious of its success, other teams started to do the same.

Cook had by now left Walpamur Paints in murky circumstances. The company became aware he was selling paint 'on the side', having it sent out but failing to put in invoices. He wound up in the Melbourne Magistrates' Court charged with theft, receiving a $100, twelve-month good behaviour bond on 2 February 1978. Norm Goss appeared to give character evidence.

Cook quickly landed a position in promotions with Puma. Ken Mitchell, who'd brought Puma to Australia in 1970, enticed him to the company. Paying well, with flexible hours, a generous expense account and a company car, it was a cushy job. He would go in to the office at Keys Road, Moorabbin in the morning, push around some paperwork, make a few phone calls, then spend the rest of the day on the road, his car loaded with Puma products.

There were also interstate trips, to Brisbane to meet Rugby League champion Wally Lewis, and to Perth to catch up with champion cricketers Dennis Lillee and Bruce Yardley.

His main responsibility was to tie up deals with sportsmen and sportswomen. By being seen in Puma, they gave the brand invaluable exposure and credibility, particularly among youngsters keen to emulate the habits of their heroes.

The affable Cook was good at his job, pressing Puma footwear and apparel onto footballers, cricketers, rugby players, basketballers, netballers, and hockey and soccer players. He had about thirty-five percent of league footballers decked out in Puma.

'I had carte blanche to walk into virtually any changing room in any Australian sport,' Cook says.

His mate and former coach Ted Whitten was doing the same role at rival Adidas. On occasion, they were tussling over the same sportsman. But they made sure they were never played off against each other, happy to tell one another what they were paying the star.

Cook had also started doing sportsman's nights, accepting gigs all over Victoria. He would walk in with his Puma goods and give them away. 'All good PR,' he says. He also judged a Puma player of the week in *The Sporting Globe*, giving the winner a bag and boots.

League footballers Peter Knights, John Hendrie and Barry Rowlings, and former Victorian cricketer Nigel Murch, were on the Puma payroll at the same time as Cook. Rowlings says Cook was 'a natural' in the role, profiting from his profile. 'He was a legend back then,' Rowlings says. 'Everyone knew Fred.'

On one occasion, Cook was put with a puma for a publicity shot. The animal latched on to him, drawing blood. The shoot resumed after he was cleaned up, the promotions manager smiling broadly but holding the large cat tight to prevent another attack.

As he often points out, Cook made a fortune not out of football, but because of it. He was a champion networker as well as a champion goalkicker, taking care to shake hands and share a story with 'the powers that be'. As he discovered, some people, even executives at big companies, could go ga-ga in the presence of public figures.

But Cook was also mindful of giving time to the man in the street. He always remembered what Ted Whitten had said to him: you could talk to nine out of ten people, but the one you brushed would always be sore about it.

'They'd say, "Oh, that Fred Cook wouldn't talk to me." I never wanted that on my conscience, that I'd ignored somebody,' Cook says. 'Because I had my own heroes when I was growing up and I knew how much they meant to me, your Charlie Suttons and Ted Whittens.'

9

TO understand Fred Cook's fame, it's necessary to understand the hold the VFA had on football watchers in the 1970s. These were the halcyon days of a competition that for many years lived in the shadow of the league (ironically, the league was formed from breakaway association clubs at the end of 1896).

Many credit the resurgence of the VFA to Channel 0 starting to televise matches in 1967, highlighting fierce suburban rivalries and playing up the more rugged aspects of matches.

Phil Cleary says that when he first played for Coburg in 1975, the VFA was a 'Melbourne ritual which looked to have been plucked from Nero's colosseum'. The telecasts became 'compulsive viewing'.

In his history of the VFA, Marc Fiddian wrote that officials had coveted TV coverage as a means of keeping up with the VFL. There was 'absolution elation' when Channel 0 decided to stop covering the league and go with the association.

'Channel 0 had the field to itself, although it was taking a risk by totally committing to the second tier of Melbourne football,' Fiddian wrote. 'The biggest factor in the television channel's favour was Sunday and there were no counter attractions to prevent it capturing a big audience. The success was immediate and Channel 0 tapped a market that would not have otherwise been interested in the VFA. People were enthusiastic about what they saw and in a lot of cases decided to attend games at Port Melbourne, Preston, Sandringham, Toorak Park, Dandenong and so on.'

Phil Gibbs, now eighty-six and living on a three-and-a-half acre property forty kilometres north of Launceston, was Channel 0 sports director and anchored the coverage, working alongside Ted Henry and Craig Kelly.

From the outset, he told cameramen to concentrate on close-up shots of the players, wanting viewers to recognise them before their names were called. He was keen to highlight their personalities as much as their play, and make them welcome figures in lounge rooms. Setting the template for future broadcasters, Channel 0 also interviewed coaches and players on the boundary line, quizzing them on the status of the match and checking in on injuries and reports.

Gibbs also had VFA officials ban cars from parking around grounds, believing they made the competition look like country football. He wanted a 'fair dinkum product'.

Gibbs happily admits he encouraged a brand of 'good, tough, hard football' at a time when the league was trying to clean up the game. Before one match, big Bob Johnson, then in charge of Oakleigh, asked him if there was anything he could do to help with the day's coverage.

'Well, it would be nice if you could thump some poor bastard in the first quarter,' Gibbs replied. 'That will give us an audience to work with.'

Gibbs says the players were happy to play up to the cameras, knowing it helped attract ratings and popularise their competition.

Channel 0 was on a commercial break when one fight broke out. Gibbs sent word to the boundary that it would be nice if it could flare up again when it was back on air. Soon there were more fisticuffs. A newspaper advertisement from 1970 gave an insight into the station's promotion of the broadcast. It showed a Port Melbourne player face down on the ground, surrounded by teammates, Sandringham opponents and umpires. 'Remember when Port Melbourne and Sandringham last met … This Sunday it will be on again … on ATV Channel 0.'

Gibbs was criticised by league authorities, including Jack Hamilton, for encouraging what they viewed as violence.

'She was a tough old game,' Gibbs says. 'But it wasn't violent. A punch-up here and there was part and parcel of VFA football. The VFL was trying to take away the hard knocks. We were trying to get them in. It didn't worry me what Jack said. My whole outlook was about getting the television station good ratings. That's what we set out to do, and we got 'em. To me it proved a point, and that is that people don't mind a bit of rough stuff on a football field. Now it's a hanging offence. The kids today wouldn't know what a shirt-front was!'

In 1979, Gibbs was caught up in an episode that left him shaken. After a thrilling match at Geelong West, Roosters and Port Melbourne supporters brawled under the Channel 0 van. Gibbs was subjected to abuse and threats, apparently for selecting Port to win. The Roosters triumphed by three points, despite five goals from Cook. 'It was truly frightening that day, dealing with such a wild mob,' Gibbs recalls. 'There was no way we were going back to Geelong West without police protection.'

As for Cook, he says the Port Melbourne full forward often played up to the cameras and enjoyed being the VFA's biggest drawcard. When it appeared the match of the day would be one-sided, Gibbs would take Cook aside and ask him to pull out something extra: a bag of goals, a few spectacular marks or to exaggerate the effect of any hit he received.

More than once Cook stayed on the ground for longer than necessary before groggily shaking his head and getting to his feet. He pulled it off so well he could have left the ground, showered and walked onstage at the Princess Theatre, there to play wounded hero. He would also take snaps from the boundary line, his eye on the prize of goal of the day.

Gibbs and Cook became friends, often sharing a drink after games. 'He gave me a lot of copy, Fred. He was a fantastic footballer and a good team man,' Gibbs says. 'In my book, if you want to be a good footballer you've first and foremost got to be a good team man, just like Gary Ablett is at the moment.'

Triple Port Melbourne premiership coach Gary Brice says Cook was integral to the broadcast. In his mind, the full forward was the VFA. 'The cameras would always be zooming in on him. He was exactly what they needed at the time. People would tune in just to watch him and see how many he would kick.'

Gibbs fumed when the VFA put its TV coverage out to tender at the end of the 1978 season, believing Channel 0 had strengthened the association's position in its battle to hold ground against the VFL. He told *The Herald* the station had taken a risk in beginning to televise the competition a decade earlier. 'I think Channel 0 can rightly claim a great deal of credit for some of the success the VFA now enjoys,' he said.

Channel 0 had paid $168,000 for the previous contract, but Gibbs said he would recommend it drop the coverage. It continued its weekly broadcast until 1981, although it did cover finals in the following years (the ABC's telecast began in 1988).

At the same time, the association was moving towards cleaning up an image that had served it well. An order-off rule was introduced in 1980, and renowned hard man Trevor Price, playing for Werribee, was the first player sent from the ground, by umpire Frank Vergona.

Gibbs always told VFA officials that the league, jealous of the following the association had built, would try to muscle in on Sunday broadcasts. He thought the VFL would quickly win bigger audiences because of its superior standard of football. He read the play like Brownlow Medal champion Greg Williams. First league reserves games in 1979 (playing for the Commodore Cup) and then matches televised out of Sydney weakened the VFA's grip on Sunday football.

'Once they came in, that was the end of the VFA,' Gibbs says. 'They were shot to bits.'

When the league began to talk about playing on Sundays, Cook used his column in *The Sporting Globe*, 'Up Forward', to attack the proposal.

Writing in 1977, he said it sounded like a great idea — 'for the VFL.' 'Apart from themselves, they haven't taken much else into consideration.' He said it had been proven the league and association couldn't survive playing on the same day. By the time Cook finished playing in 1985, the VFA had seen its most robust days.

In 2013, Gibbs received life membership of the Australian Football Media Association for his 'lasting and significant' contribution to the game. Eddie McGuire, who cut his calling teeth in the VFA alongside Gibbs, presented him with the award.

Reminded that he also called with Bruce McAvaney, Gibbs quickly replies: 'Get it right — he called with me!' But he's proud of the influence Channel 0 had on the VFA, helping thrust it into the limelight for more than a decade.

ı|| ı

IN 1977, Cook was being referred to not only as the champion Port Melbourne footballer, but a 'media personality'. On Fridays he was part of the panel for the 3DB sports lunches and on Saturdays he served on the radio station's around-the-grounds team, going to league matches and providing score updates.

He also had his column in *The Sporting Globe*, ghost written by Michael Lovett, now editor of the *AFL Record*. Cook's photo byline featured alongside football scribe Greg Hobbs, racing writers Rollo Roylance and Shane Templeton, and boxing expert Merv Williams.

Lovett would phone Cook and they would cover off players, teams and issues of the day. 'It was nothing too controversial or hard-hitting,' Lovett says. 'I think he played a fairly straight bat. We did it on the back of how popular he was at the time. He was probably like what Andrew Gaze was to basketball.'

At league finals time, *The Globe* used Cook as an analyst — a VFA player commenting on the VFL! — for the Saturday edition. Before games, Lovett and Cook would meet at the Hilton Hotel, and Lovett remembers Cook being swamped by admirers on the short walk to the MCG.

'There would be people grabbing him, saying, "Fred, we love ya,"' Lovett says. 'He'd be signing autographs and patting kids on the head and saying, "G'day champ, how are ya?" There was a bit of rock star about him. And it's fair to say he lapped it all up.'

Sam Newman uses a similar term to describe Cook's standing at the time. He says he was a 'pop star' and a 'man about town' people sought out for company.

Newman says it was staggering that Cook rose to such prominence after playing so little league football. 'He went from a bloke who played a few games for Footscray, to an absolute hero and the figurehead of

VFA football,' he says. 'He almost singlehandedly put the broadcasting of the VFA on the map. He was a genuine drawcard. The crowds he could pull hadn't been seen before and haven't been since.'

The Globe also used Cook as 'Freddie at the ready' to interview other sporting stars. He chatted with women's tennis fashion designer Ted Tinling, being sized up for a pair of blue shorts with red flowers.

Grappling with wrestler Bruno Sammartino, he was pictured in a headlock and about to be body-slammed into the canvas. 'I've wrestled a few full backs in my time, but none were built like this big hunk,' he opened his account.

And he sat next to an exhausted and ill Tony Rafferty after his attempt to run a world-record 1600 kilometres.

Then there were the sportsman's nights. He usually did two or three every week, pocketing $300 for each.

The thought of getting up before a crowd that was expecting to be entertained initially made him anxious. He worried about hecklers. But he quickly realised he could control most situations with the microphone in his hand. If a drunk got up and tried to interject, Cook would cut him down with the words, 'Don't worry folks, he just wants to let everyone know he's a poofter. But that's okay, we're among friends here.'

He worked particularly well with Newman. Cook maintains the US actor Jack Klugman, visiting Melbourne in the early 1980s, heard them speak at a function at Moonee Valley Racecourse and was so impressed he said he could arrange a thirteen-week contract for them in Las Vegas.

They would do their homework before gigs. If they were speaking at a football club they would find out the names of the star players and the coach, and ask for a suitable target, a 'bunny' upon whom they could pin a few put-down lines.

Newman has fond recollections of their time on the speaking circuit, calling them the 'halcyon days of drinking too much' and 'having too much of a good time'.

'You wouldn't get away with it today, because you can't have a drink and get in the car and drive. Not that we used to drive when we were alcoholically propelled, but we're a lot a more careful these days,' Newman says. 'But the functions Fred and I would go to were actually an interruption to the night we had planned. We'd get it out of the way and get on with the night.'

As for the Klugman offer, he says: 'He might have said that to Fred. I don't know if that's apocryphal or not, but we certainly did meet Jack Klugman. I think he was bemused by us more than anything. But if Fred said Jack told him we were both stars, who am I to argue?'

Cook, Newman says, would take a modicum of truth and embellish it to something unrecognisable from fact. He would tone it down in a sort of good cop/bad cop act.

Former Port Melbourne player Brendan Behan says Cook's reach was remarkable for a VFA player. 'Back then, Freddie was much bigger than Sam Newman,' Behan says. 'He was a celebrity in his own way. It was quite something, and showed the strength of his personality and probably the stature of the VFA.'

Cook even accompanied the wrestler Andre the Giant on a tour to regional Victoria, watching him steadily empty twenty-six large bottles of beer as he drank with Ted Whitten, who was on gin and tonic. When the liquor got the better of Whitten, the great wrestler gently picked him up, tucked him under an arm and announced: 'I put Ted to bed. I think Ted tired.'

There was also an occasion when a suburban sports club ran a promotion for junior cricketers: come along, kids, and win a bike by bowling out Fred Cook. He saw among the youngsters a boy wearing calipers and decided he had to have the bike. When he finally landed a ball on the stumps, Cook took a wild swipe and was bowled. The lad with the calipers was overjoyed. The other boys sensed a set-up.

Cook took on a lot of commitments. But he says he always made the time to work on his football, knowing it was the goals and the premierships that created his openings off the field.

'Footy underpinned the whole shebang,' he says. 'It was always my priority. Everything revolved around it. I always thought I was one bad game away from a fall. It could all come crashing down, just like that.'

ı|lı

IN 1978, Cook totted up a ton, his fourth on the spin, resting on 115 goals to head the association list for the third consecutive time. He ticked into triple figures with a return of ten against Caulfield.

In Norm Brown's mind, Cook was well established as the best player in the VFA, his marking making him a nigh unstoppable force in the forward line. He'd also grown into a leader, recognised with the captaincy.

'Cookie was easy to coach,' Brown says. 'He knew the rules. He knew what he had to do. I gave him a pretty free licence. He was like a tin of worms — here, there and everywhere — but he was such a great player. If I needed a whipping boy at three-quarter time, if he was having a day when he wouldn't chase out of defence, he'd cop it sweet. If you'd asked any coach in the VFA at that time which player they'd want from another club, they'd have said Fred. He was a big forward, regularly kicking 100-plus goals. He'd put the icing on the cake.'

He says the only time Cook tested his patience was before games, when he'd have a cup of tea with the ladies in the Port Melbourne canteen and be late to strip. 'He was bloody hopeless in that regard!'

Brown is adamant Cook could have passed 200 goals in a season if he'd been a better kick. Seasoned Port Melbourne supporters have not forgotten how he missed a goal from the top of the square in 1978, costing the Borough victory against South Adelaide in an NFL Escort Cup night series match at South Melbourne. His teammates were mortified; the club had agreed they could split any prize money. 'He wouldn't have been ten yards out,' Bob Profitt remembers. 'He shrugged his shoulders and said, "Oh well, that's football." We were ropeable!'

But Cook's mere presence produced many goals. Brown saw teams double and sometimes triple-team his spearhead, but it worked to Port's advantage: the spoiling efforts of backmen created scoring opportunities for small men like Holt and Harland.

Brown had retired from playing during the 1977 season, closing a career that years later would be crowned with selection in Fitzroy's team of the century. Even without the big fellow, Port Melbourne earned the minor premiership, with thirteen wins and five losses.

But the finals brought two defeats, by four points to Preston in the second semi, and by twenty-two points to eventual premier Prahran in the preliminary final. Cook kicked four goals, but the equally flamboyant Sam Kekovich slotted five for the True Blues, who trailed by twenty-four points early in the last quarter.

Cook says the club took it hard. Port Melbourne expected rather than hoped to win in September, and it was unacceptable to be bounced out in successive weeks.

'Maybe it was complacency,' Cook says. 'Maybe we thought we'd just roll up and do what we'd done before. Doesn't work like that.

When you're the benchmark the other teams set themselves for you, want to get your scalp. Doesn't matter if it's a racehorse or a runner or a swimmer, it's a pretty sharp point at the top. Not easy to stay there.'

At the start of the season, Cook was ringing alarm bells about Port Melbourne. A few Port players, he declared in his *Globe* column, 'must come back to earth'.

'Some players and supporters are running around with the idea that we are odds-on to win the flag again,' he wrote. 'Well if you took practice match form into account I'd say a more realistic price would be 50–1. One of the problems is that some players don't realise last year's premiership celebrations have finished.'

In the same column he noted that his former Port premiership teammate Mick Erwin had revitalised Prahran and it would be a big improver. They were more prescient words.

Brown went on the players' trip away to Queensland and stayed on for an extra week. When he returned to Melbourne he learned through one of his players that Port Melbourne had decided to advertise the coaching position. He was annoyed; he'd already started planning recruiting for 1979.

'Yes, I got the "Khyber Pass",' he says. 'They decided to tender for my job. The excuse was they wanted a playing coach and it was in their constitution. It was disappointing. I would have preferred they'd told me earlier. If it had been handled better it would have been more palatable. To find out that way …'

Brown could look back on five seasons that brought three premierships and two other finals appearances, one of Port's most successful periods. It was, he says, a great time to be involved at the Borough. 'I've always said I met some of the best people I've ever met at Port and I also met some of the worst people I've ever met. And half the time they were related!'

Cook ruled the goal square at Port Melbourne. But a player whose goalkicking record and profile far exceeded his own was on his way to the Borough as playing coach for the 1979 season.

ı|lı

PETER McKenna was Collingwood royalty. Owning the truest of boots, he was the Magpies' leading goalkicker every year from 1967 to 1974, stacking up 838 goals in 180 games, with centuries in 1970 (143), 1971 (134) and 1972 (130).

And when he wasn't cutting up full backs he was cutting records, releasing the singles 'Things to Remember' and 'Smile' in the early 1970s. His handsome looks and floppy fringe often had him described in Beatlesque terms. McKenna was a boy soprano. When he reached adulthood, he says, 'I could sing in tune, that's about it.' At Collingwood social nights he always sang 'Galway Bay'.

McKenna also had a stint on the entertainment program *Hey Hey It's Saturday* before Collingwood, worried it would detract from his form, put a stop to it.

'He was huge at his peak, as big as anyone in the game, a pin-up boy,' seasoned football writer Geoff Poulter says of McKenna. 'There was McKenna, Alex Jesaulenko and probably Royce [Hart].'

After finishing with the Magpies in 1975, McKenna had one-year stops at Devonport, Carlton and Geelong West. He kicked sixty-seven goals for the Roosters in 1978, but decided to retire.

Port Melbourne intervened. The Borough were poised to appoint former St Kilda and Melbourne centreman Glenn Elliott as coach, but the deal fell through, as did talks with former Carlton player Phil Pinnell. Port officials contacted McKenna, saying the club needed a captain-coach — and quickly. McKenna hadn't been training and was reluctant to accept the job.

'No, I didn't want to coach. I didn't. I'd given it away,' he says. 'But they asked me and asked me. I discussed it with my wife for a couple of days, and because they were such a great club I decided to have a go at it. But deep down, I didn't want to do it.'

McKenna was reunited with his former Collingwood teammate John Greening and could also select 1970 Brownlow Medal champion Peter Bedford, who had returned to Port twelve months earlier, and mid-season inclusion Rod Carter, who later gave the Sydney Swans many years of staunch service at full back.

McKenna and Cook played on each other briefly in a league match at Victoria Park, and McKenna was aware of his remarkable goalkicking feats in the VFA. He decided to leave Cook in his preferred position. But he was less productive than in previous seasons, finishing fourth on the list with seventy-nine goals from eighteen matches, including ten in Round 3. Smith and Radojevic shared top billing with ninety-seven. McKenna slotted fifty-two from fourteen outings.

As with the previous season, the Borough were bested in the preliminary final, losing to Geelong West by thirty points.

McKenna remembers the match well. 'There was a howling north wind blowing down the ground at Junction Oval,' he says. 'We were kicking with the wind, and in the first five minutes of the game Joe Radojevic kicked two goals against this gale. We were chasing our arse a bit because we didn't have a big enough lead at quarter time. But if we had've got through Geelong West we would have beaten [premier] Coburg in the grand final for sure.'

Cook struggled on accomplished Roosters full back Jan Smith, to the point he went to the bench in the last quarter. McKenna kicked five goals, almost answering Radojevic's six for West.

'I dragged Fred. He'd hardly had a bloody kick on Jan Smith,' McKenna recalls. 'I had to do something, you know. I don't think he was very happy with me about that. Freddie had trouble with Jan Smith. He could beat everyone else, but he always seemed to have problems on him.'

Not entirely true, Cook says, recalling decent returns on the Rooster. He regarded Smith as a fine and fair player, but he rated Prahran's hard-spoiling Kerry Foley as the best full back who opposed him, believing he'd had a good match if he kicked four goals on the former Collingwood player.

Smith, who was on Geelong's list in 1980 and 1981, and Fitzroy's in 1982, says it was a daunting task to play on Cook. He was strong and almost impossible to shift from his position, marked everything, was quick on the lead and fought hard at ground level (a feature of his days as a defender at Footscray).

Smith always tried to stand off Cook and jump and spoil from behind or the side. 'He was a huge man. You couldn't wrestle him,' he says. 'Getting a bit of a leap was the best way to go about it, I found.' He regards his performance on Cook in the 1979 preliminary final as one of the best of his career.

In 1983, after returning to Geelong West from the Roys, Smith was reported in the finals series. He asked Cook to provide character evidence at the tribunal hearing. Cook even drove him there, showing off the mobile phone (then a novelty) in his car. Smith beat the report.

Cook enjoyed his season under McKenna. But he's always believed that McKenna, on leaving the huddle, would whisper instructions to players to pass the ball to him since he was a far better kick. 'Well that's bullshit, you know,' McKenna responds. 'You know that's a bullshit story.'

He says Cook gave him unstinting support during his term — and loads of laughs. 'Great character, Freddie. Never a dull moment when he was around, that's for sure.'

Cook says it was a high-profile appointment for the club, but McKenna handled the team less surely than Brown, owing to his inexperience. 'He wasn't the first and he won't be the last champion footballer not cut out for coaching,' Cook says. As for having two full forwards in one team, he says, 'It probably didn't work out … too much conflict … I wasn't sure if the ball was being kicked to me or Peter.'

In his excellent history of Port Melbourne, *A Different Breed*, long-time Borough watcher Terry Keenan expressed the view the Cook–McKenna forward set-up did not work. He said McKenna's appointment 'smacked of desperation'.

The former Magpie champion, he said, 'was an out and out full forward and in Fred Cook Port already had perhaps the best full forward seen in modern VFA history'. He went on to say, 'As a result of this appointment the balance of the team was jeopardised, not to mention the possibility of tensions surrounding the natural rivalry about who was to be the main attacking focus in the team.'

For his part, McKenna says there was no rivalry with Cook. He didn't care who kicked the goals, as long as Port Melbourne kicked enough to win games.

One of Cook's best performances for the season came when captaining the VFA team against Queensland at Prahran. Both he and Kim Smith kicked seven goals in a thumping victory. Norm Goss said it was the best association representative side he'd seen.

The highlight of Port's season came on J. J. Liston Trophy night, when Vic Aanensen became the club's first winner since its other great ruckman, Frank Johnson, in 1952.

Aanensen's background was typical of many Port players of the time. He lived in Ross Street, not far from North Port Oval, played juniors with Port YMCA and joined the Port Melbourne thirds. Serving a classical apprenticeship, he did his time in the seconds before earning his senior stripes.

A stop with South Melbourne produced forty senior games from 1973 to 1976. On returning to the Borough, he became one of the most dominant big men in the VFA, powerfully built but mobile. Aanensen would also win the 1981 Liston. By the time he left Port before the 1982 season, he'd played in three premierships and nabbed three best and fairests.

As for his nickname, he was walking down Bay Street with a friend when a passerby, no doubt noting the schoolboy's height, called him 'Stretch'. It stuck like gum on a shoe.

McKenna had only one season at Port Melbourne, stepping down to take up a position in the commentary box for Channel 7, where he called for twenty years. But there was one more kick in his career. His old pal Colin Hobbs enticed him to Northcote in 1980; dashing off to matches after his *World of Sport* commitments, he booted ninety-eight goals.

Cook's 1979 return of seventy-nine goals had some VFA watchers questioning if, at age thirty-one, his best football was in the past. *Herald* scribe John Craven even said his career had reached a crossroads, describing Cook's performance against Geelong West in the preliminary final as 'pitiful'. He'd been humiliated when McKenna dragged him from the ground.

'Cook, a VFA goalscoring freak, has two problems,' Craven said. 'The first is that he turns thirty-two in November. The second — and it's far more important than the first — is that he has got by in his VFA career on sheer natural ability. Cook freely admits that he has never had to dedicate himself to the game like other lesser lights. But with the ageing process creeping up on him he found last week that the gifts he possesses did not compensate for what can best be described as a lack of fitness.'

Unless he knuckled down over summer and displayed more dedication, his career would come to a sudden halt, Craven declared. The VFA could ill afford to lose a player 'with the personality and drawing power of the 1970 J. J. Liston Trophy winner'. Craven said, 'It is hoped that he responds and subjects his mind and body to a vigorous program of fitness and discipline over the next few months.'

Cook didn't need the advice. The numbers told the tale. He was so disappointed with his 1979 season that he began training the day after the loss to Geelong West, determined to show his form had been a blip rather than the start of a decline.

ı|ı

THEY called him 'Barrel' because it aptly described his upper body. Gary Brice was a barrel-chested, powerful man, showing as much over 171 games for South Melbourne from the first to last seasons of the 1970s.

He was an equally strong leader of men, as Fred Cook was to discover after Brice had been appointed to replace McKenna.

Cook himself had applied for the position, encouraged by Norm Goss to stick in an application. He was unfussed when he missed out; he didn't know where he would have found the time.

'The club did the right thing when they made Bricey coach. Not only were they getting a champion player, they were getting a coach,' Cook says. 'Worked out pretty well, didn't it? He had a little bit of success, didn't he?'

Three premierships worth, in fact. Brice steered Port Melbourne to the 1980, 1981 and 1982 flags, the first time the club had secured such a hat-trick.

When the Borough named their team of the century in 2003, they named 'Barrel' as an interchange player, but also as coach. It was one position about which there was no debate.

The premierships were won under different circumstances. In 1980, Port fabulously and famously hurried home to defeat Coburg. The following year, it caned Preston by 113 points. In 1982, it defeated Preston again, when the Bullants were a hot favourite and Brice was guiding a team that was thought to be past its best.

Cook gave his coach sterling service, with returns of 112 in 1980, 106 in 1981 and 139 in 1982. Although past the age of thirty, he remained a formidable forward, his hands more clamping than marking the ball.

Cook holds up the 1980 grand final as one of the most cherished days of his long career. Many years later, he can recall its turning points, the small moments that contributed to a victory that looked beyond the Borough. He'd gone into the match with another century of goals, achieved with a return of four against Coburg in the final round, but also a twisted ankle.

'Before I ran out I had seven or eight injections, so I couldn't feel it. I had ten metres of tape holding it together,' Cook says. 'I was also on the pink mix — liquid morphine and Aspirin. I was supposed to have a teaspoon, but I was drinking it like a cold can of beer. Anything to get out there and be able to take a few catches and kick some goals.'

Coburg, coached by Colin Kinnear, lost only twice in the home-and-away games, both times to Port. And it fell to the Borough by fifty points in the second semi-final.

But at three-quarter time in the grand final, it appeared the Lions would take the match that counted. They led by seventeen points and had held Port to only five goals. Ten minutes into the last quarter, their advantage was twenty points.

All over? Brice knew his team never gave up, was superbly fit and would have a finishing kick, despite working into the wind. Jim Christou and Tony Ebeyer slotted goals to unsettle Coburg, then goals from Glyn Evans and Christou stripped it of the lead. Port had no business to be in front, but it was.

Now Cook got involved, taking a pass from Ebeyer. He had kicked three goals and double the number of points. His ankle was playing up. The pain was so bad that after marking he had to use the ball as a prop to get to his feet.

'I'd been missing them,' Cook says. 'Because of the wind I worked out I had to kick the ball three or four metres out of bounds to the left-hand side. So I let it go. When it came off the boot people thought, *Aww shit, he's missed again … hang on, wait, it's coming back, it's coming back*. It went through dead fuckin' centre.'

Brice remembers that it looked like the ball was heading to Bass Strait. 'That was a team-lifter, that one. He wasn't the longest or straightest kick, but he's gone back and let it go from forty-five metres, and got it through. I was running back to the centre and he said, "What do you think, coach?" And I said, "It's about beeping time."'

Port was eleven points to the good, and Billy Swan helped preserve the lead by running down Coburg forward David Fisher just as he steadied to kick at an open goal. There was only a finger in it, a Swan finger that caught in the back of Fisher's shorts.

Appropriately, Christou ensured the flag would be hoisted at North Port Oval, booting his third goal of the quarter, after a zigzagging dash that started out of the centre and finished with a spearing fifty-metre kick.

'We played one quarter of football and won the flag? How good are we?' bubbled Norm Goss to pressmen.

Cook likens Port's comeback to a cigarette lighter starting to run low on gas. 'We kept flicking and flicking at it until we got a spark and a flame. Once we got that run-on, all the year's work seemed to come together.'

But Cook was violently ill after the match. The morphine–Aspirin concoction he had guzzled repeated on him. 'I had this black liquid coming out of my stomach, a heap of it. I keeled over in the toilet with all this black shit coming out of my mouth. Never been so crook in my life.'

Kinnear felt a little sick too, having seen victory snatched from his team. But, just as the vanquished Bob Bonnett did after Kinnear coached a reserves team to a grand final victory over Port a few years earlier, he made a point of going into the Borough rooms and extending congratulations.

He says his team gave it everything, but in the end ran out of manpower. 'We'd won the premiership in 1979, beating Geelong West, and that day we came from something like thirty-eight points down,' Kinnear says. 'In 1980, it went the other way. We were up but we couldn't run the game out, and in the end Port were too good for us. We missed a goal early in the last quarter that would have put us four goals in front. But after that the game went too long for us. If there had been a fifth quarter, Port would have won by twenty-five, thirty points.'

Cook, he says, was 'just a wonderful player' and almost impossible to stop in sixteen-a-side football. There were no wingmen to drop back and fill in holes across half back.

'When you played full back on Fred Cook, the ball was coming in at different angles and with a lot of open space in between,' Kinnear says. 'He was very strong above his head, Cookie, and he didn't miss many marks. When he did you'd have all those smaller guys coming in, the Christous, the Harlands, the Holts, the Ebeyers, to feed off him.'

Given he later coached the Sydney Swans, Kinnear is well qualified to judge whether Cook could have been a successful spearhead in league football.

'No doubt whatsoever,' Kinnear says. 'In his early days in footy, Fred played at centre half back, so he had the mobility, he had the height, he had the ability to win the ball. He didn't have to have the ball kicked down his throat to get the ball. He'd win it in the air because he was rarely going to be outmarked. You only have to imagine how he would have been on a ground like North Melbourne, or later at the SCG when the ball's coming down at 100 miles an hour. Marvellous footballer, Cookie.'

Norm Goss junior and David Holt shared Kinnear's view. Having roved for South Melbourne on Saturdays, Goss would watch his old club on Sundays and, like many supporters, marvel at Cook's performances.

'He was a terrific mark, a one-grab mark, and a good body player,' Goss says. 'He was a terrible kick, of course — he could have kicked a lot more goals. But he got better with his kicking. He got into a routine, and he wasn't too bad from thirty yards out. Anything more than that would test him. But I always thought Fred could play full forward in the VFL. No doubt. I know he was a lot better than some of the blokes we had at full forward at South Melbourne.'

Holt believes Cook would have been a seventy-goal forward if he went back to the VFL. 'He had a great pair of hands and he was so strong,' he says. 'I know he would have held his own.'

Crowning Port's 1980 season, twenty-year-old key forward Steve Allender claimed the J. J. Liston Trophy. A nephew of the great Peter Bedford, Allender had been working at Telecom on the day of the count, when Port secretary Jack McFarlane phoned and said he needed to attend the presentation at the Palais. He rushed around for a suit, rounded up his girlfriend Annette Townsend, and won with five votes to spare.

They returned to the family home to have a cup of tea with his parents and siblings. At 11pm there was a knock at the door. It was Cook and a few others, slabs of beer slung over their shoulders. A party started in the lounge room. It made Allender's night even more memorable. He'd adored Cook and as a schoolboy snaffled his autograph. 'That's probably the best memory I have of that night — drinking with the great Freddie Cook,' he says. 'It was probably my introduction to alcohol.'

Allender had made only two senior appearances before the start of the year. By the end of it he was earning glowing notices. 'He runs like a deer, takes a mark Peter Knights would be proud of and kicks the ball out of sight,' was how football writer Michael Lovett described him. He went to South Melbourne in 1981 and played twenty-eight senior matches before transferring to Hawthorn in 1984.

Allender was one of a number of young players Brice had entrusted with senior positions in 1980. When he accepted the coaching job, Brice thought Port could be in for a 'rebuilding phase', having lost players of the calibre of Rod Carter, Peter Bedford, Peter McKenna, John Greening, Tony Haenen and former Bulldog David Thorpe.

But he replaced experience with youth. Allender, fellow tall forward Grant O'Riley, Peter Wilkinson, Ebeyer, Shane Doyle and

Frank Johnson (son of the legendary ruckman Frank) came into the team and flourished, the mid-season acquisitions of Swans pair Terry O'Neill and Peter Hall fortified a shaky backline, and Jim Christou had returned, joining his brother John.

But did the Borough have enough to beat Coburg? At the last change in the grand final, it crossed Brice's mind that he might be looking for a new job in 1981.

What followed, he says, was a 'magnificent effort' and a snapshot of the pride of Port Melbourne Football Club.

'We couldn't have asked any more from them. They didn't stop having a go,' Brice reflects. 'When I think of where we were at the halfway stage of the season — after nine games were 6–3 and not playing great footy — it was a remarkable turnaround. The desire that day was something else.'

ı|||ı

IF the Borough only just scraped through in 1980, they waltzed home the following year.

After finishing four games on top of the ladder, they hammered Preston by seventy-one points in the second semi-final, and buried the Bullants by an even greater margin in the grand final. As with the previous year, there was a J. J. Liston Trophy to accompany the Port premiership, with champion big man Aanensen winning his second in three years. Anderson, back from Collingwood, kicked four goals in the grand final, Aanensen controlled the ruck and Peter Bradbury gave notice of his potential as a running defender. He would go on to be a premiership player under Kevin Sheedy at Essendon in 1984.

Cook, once more relishing the big stage, booted eight of Port's thirty-two goals, in the process clocking up his one hundredth for the season. A photograph of him appeared in *The Age* next day: he was bare-chested, his fringe was wet with sweat and in his right hand he held a bottle of champagne and a can of beer. He was surrounded by supporters.

'We were clearly the best team in it that year,' recalls centreman Billy Swan. 'Best side by a mile, really.'

Legendary Port Melbourne figure Tommy Lahiff declared it the best team to represent Port in twenty years.

Brice says it would have been an 'absolute disaster' if his side hadn't defeated Preston. The margin was a blow-out, but the Bullants trailed by only five points at half time. Brice pulled what he calls one of the best moves of his coaching career: he took himself off the ground. He enjoyed what he saw from the interchange bench. A tough contest dissolved into a Borough training drill. 'Everything we did paid off,' Brice says. 'It was one of those days you wished came along more often. Sensational.'

Brice was calm and considered during the week, but an occasionally volcanic character on match days, his former players say. 'He would have his moments. He could give a spray. Once that siren went he got a little bit of white line fever in him, I suppose,' Swan says.

Cook says Brice was intent on making the most of the players he had. He set high standards and it was unacceptable when they weren't met.

'Has was a hard disciplinarian. He never wavered on that. He could give a bloody good spray, Bricey,' Cook says. 'He'd be frothing at the mouth after he'd finished. Didn't matter if you were a young kid who needed to be knocked into line or if you were a senior player getting slack, you'd get a barrage. But he led by example. I think he became a harder player when he became captain and coach of Port Melbourne.'

He says he and Brice had one thing in common: 'We were both shit-frightened of Old Man Goss!' Brice adds, 'And we weren't the only two.'

Pushing up players such as Brendan Kavanagh, Russell Davies and Andy Demetriou to maintain enthusiasm, Brice drove his squad hard ahead of the 1981 season. He was determined to crush even a hint of complacency. The players became fitter and their skills went to another level.

'I'm sure they thought I was a lunatic at times. I probably was,' Brice says with a laugh. 'But I wanted to make sure there wouldn't be any slackening off.'

Even his now-veteran full forward, never the greatest trainer, was pushed. When he took the job, Brice was warned that he might have trouble with Cook, who occasionally skipped or was late for training, owing to his busy work schedule. Coach told the player he needed him to be at every session. There could be no exceptions.

From time to time, Cook was late on the track as he opened the boot of his car and flogged off Puma products, always a nice on-the-side earn for him.

Michael Lovett remembers attending a Port training session and seeing Cook dispensing his wares. 'Fred, is there any chance you're going to join us tonight?' an exasperated Brice asked.

Brice regarded Cook as a proud man and would pick at his pride to get the best from him. At a Saultry running session, for example, he told Cook he was exempt from a repetition exercise, knowing he would be too embarrassed to sit it out while his teammates sweated. It also stirred his competitive juices. He was determined to run from point post to point post in less than thirty seconds. Cook needed to do it three times (with a minute of recovery in between). If he didn't, every player would have to do six of the lung-busters.

Cook got through the first two runs, but was struggling on the third. Saultry, stopwatch in hand, slowed the count to get him across the line at thirty seconds on the knocker. Cook collapsed on the ground, at which point Saultry said to Brice, 'Hey, you know he had a heart attack in 1972, don't you?' His warm-down lap was negotiated at Cliff Young pace.

Cook was the best sprinter in the club, as he would show at training when he would dash away from the small men over forty metres. That was why he was so often seen leading into space with his opponent floundering behind, sometimes even out of the Channel 0 picture. 'He was bloody quick off the mark, Fred,' Brice says. Teammates who trailed him at training were infuriated and demanded he race them again. Cook had the same reply: 'Only need to do it once, boys.'

Saultry knew all about Cook's natural speed. In the late 1960s, Footscray Football Club put on an athletics carnival and they were drawn in the same heat. Saultry had to work to shake him off.

Cook was nudged out of the competition goalkicking in 1981, beaten by Sandringham's Rex Hunt, 110 goals to 106 (Brice says inaccuracy cost him, believing he would have consistently reached 160 if his aim was straight).

During the season he eclipsed Bob Bonnett's association record of 933 goals, assuming the top perch with eight against Sandringham. 'Cook makes history as Port coasts', *The Age* headlined Marc Fiddian's report. Bonnett was at the ground and posed for a photograph with Cook, playfully putting a fist on his chin after the game. Bonnett had it framed and it sits among a display of memorabilia at his Port Melbourne home.

Phil Cleary doesn't hesitate to call Cook the greatest player he saw in the VFA. He notes his consistency, durability, ability to produce his best in big matches, and the charisma and colour he brought to the competition.

But Cleary also has reservations about Cook's career, calling him a 'big fish in a small pond'. He believes Cook should have played a lot more league football, and ultimately failed to do justice to his substantial talent. That was part of his character, he says. It was easier for him to have status in the VFA than test himself in the VFL.

'Why not try to make it in the best competition? He left the best competition too early and became comfortable in the VFA at a time when it got massive publicity and he became a folk hero,' Cleary says. 'There's an irony in the fact that that all happened and yet he fell apart as a person. Maybe there's a moral in that story. That he fell apart as a person is not inconsistent with why he left the VFL. He didn't quite have the character to stick it out.'

Cleary often watched Cook dominate matches and wondered what the point of it was. 'He was a player who should not have been playing in the VFA. He was clearly better than that. But Fred could laugh at that and say, "Oh well, so what, I became the biggest name in the VFA in the 1970s when I could have just been another run-of-the-mill VFL player." The reality was he should have done more with his football.'

Neville Stibbard, who played with Cook in Port Melbourne's 1977 premiership side, offers a different perspective of his former teammate. Stibbard has spent more than three decades in football as a respected recruiter. Unlike his great friend Norm Goss junior, he believes Cook would not have been a success as a league spearhead.

Stibbard says Cook had deficiencies in his game — most notably his kicking — that would have been exposed, particularly with the league evolving into a running game.

'I got [Port Melbourne small man] Bernie Evans across to South Melbourne, so I think my eye was pretty sound at that stage,' Stibbard says. 'Fred was a poor kick and he was playing on opponents six inches shorter than him. There were only a couple of recognised full backs around and one was Bobby Profitt, who was in the same side. Some teams used to play a ruckman on him to try to match his height.

'Look, nothing against Freddie's talent — and I don't want to sound negative or harsh against him, because he was an absolute legend of the VFA — but the ball used to be in Port's forward line all the time because it was such a dominant side. I just think the VFA, with the sixteen men a side giving him a lot of space to run into, was made for him.'

10

NORM Goss was desperately ill. Cancer was eating away at him. Despite being a non-smoker, he had it in the lungs, and although he had a great will to live, it was apparent during 1982 that it would take him sooner rather than later.

Cook was devastated to see Goss slipping away. He thought he was indestructible, and worshipped the man who called him 'pal'. Cook regarded him more as a father than a friend. He trusted him implicitly and would have done anything to please him.

The great administrator's illness served as a solemn backdrop to Port's 1982 finals effort.

Despite having farewelled Aanensen, O'Riley, Jim and John Christou, and Paul Goss, and despite key man Billy Swan battling injury, the Borough qualified third with thirteen wins and five losses, behind Preston (16–2) and Coburg (15–3). They accounted for Geelong West by sixty-two points in the first semi, then rolled Coburg by twenty points in the preliminary final. They were in another grand final.

And yet Brice saw that Port followers were happy to have gone that far. Normally the most demanding fans, they celebrated the victory over Coburg as if the club had won a premiership.

Brice's back was up. 'The thing that really motivated me was going back to the Port social club. Port supporters only like winning. They can't stand the prospect of anything else. But there was an overriding feeling of "Wow, we've done really well to come this far, it doesn't matter what happens next week". I thought, *I'm not too happy about this.*

'So at training I said, "Did any of you blokes get an impression of what happened after the game at the social club?" A couple of blokes said, "Yeah, everyone's quite happy we've got this far and they don't think we can win." That was exactly how I felt, that our own supporters were doubting if we were good enough. I said to the players, "Anyone here think we're not good enough?" and they've all gone, "Bullshit, we're a chance." I liked their attitude, and from there they trained really well.'

On the Thursday before the decider, Brice called in Richmond powerbroker Graeme Richmond to talk to his players. He has no doubt it galvanised them further.

Brice's only regret about the Richmond visit is that he didn't tape the speech for posterity. 'It was outstanding. Just about football and how at that time of the year it wasn't football any more, it was war,' he says. 'And he left beautifully. Said his thing and walked straight out the door. And everyone just sat there and thought, *Geez.* Nothing else needed to be said.'

Rover Tony Ebeyer walked up to Brice and said, 'Why can't you give talks like that?'

'Greatest speaker I've ever heard,' Ebeyer says. 'Just phenomenal.'

More than three decades haven't blurred Cook's memory of Richmond. 'He said everyone thought Preston were the best team in the comp and they'd win the premiership,' he says. 'Then he said, "But if you want to win it, you can." It opened our eyes a bit.'

But before the match, fourteen Port players needed some form of medical attention, including a few 'jabs'. The coach himself had half a dozen injections to his Achilles and started on the bench, preferring to go with the players he'd sprinkled into the side: Brett Chadband, Mark Rodda, Angie Tantsis, Glen Robertson and Bruce Davis.

Brice had maintained that Port could beat Preston if it was within two goals at half time.

It played out better than he'd hoped: Port was in front by one point, extending its advantage to seventeen in the third quarter. 'For us to have so many walking wounded and still get up was outstanding,' Brice says.

Feeling their various ailments, the Borough slowed in the final term, but held on by seven points to match the feat of Williamstown in the 1950s in winning three consecutive premierships.

Swan thought it the most satisfying of his Port flags. 'We weren't the best team during the year, but we happened to get over them in the grand final,' he says.

It was also a J. J. Liston season for crafty centreman Swan. He shared it with Preston's Geoff Austen and Dandenong's David Wenn.

He was another local boy made good. Swan played his junior football at Port Melbourne YMCA before the family moved to the northern suburbs and he joined Broadmeadows. Swan had a run with Carlton's seconds and Under 19s, before becoming a Borough halfway through the 1975 season and staking a senior position the following year alongside schoolmates Greg Dermott, Calvin Kerr, Rob Colbert, Paul Wharton and Greg Bond.

As for Cook, he kicked five goals in the grand final. 'Just an average day for me,' he quips. But it was true. He once read that five or six goals for him was like Bradman making seventy or eighty — good going, but falling short of the standards they had set and which others expected they follow.

Cook was nearing his thirty-fifth birthday. Yet he pumped out 139 goals, forty-one more than the next player on the list, Williamstown's Mark Fotheringham. He was 'Fabulous Fred' indeed, as he kicked ten against Waverley in Round 2, Geelong West in Round 6, Williamstown in Round 11, Camberwell in Round 14 and Werribee in Round 16. He also sprayed seven behinds against Willy, preventing him from topping his best haul of fourteen against Sandringham in 1976.

Cook gave a lot of credit to the players kicking the ball to him. Most, he says, could 'kick a grain of wheat up a chook's arse and not make it blink'.

It was Cook's seventh century and his fifth and last VFA goalkicking crown. Miller earned six. Years later, when the VFL introduced a medal for the season's leading goalkicker, it named it after Miller.

Port Melbourne supporters were miffed their man was overlooked. There was little doubt his off-field problems contributed to the decision. While Cook was taking drugs and attracting police attention, Miller was living quietly in the south-eastern suburbs, labouring on building sites and training his greyhounds. They were two great spearheads. Cook finished his career with 1336 goals and Miller with 883. But one ran wild. The other was solid-citizen mild.

Phil Cleary raised the issue on his website in typically trenchant terms. 'Fred Cook was the greatest player I ever played against,' he wrote. 'In the 1970s and 1980s finding an opponent for him was a nightmare for opposition coaches. When the VFA (VFL) decided to strike a medal for the leading goalkicker, it named the award the

Jim "Frosty" Miller Medal. Frosty was a legend of the VFA but it was Cook who was the real doyen of forwards. And although the VFA said Miller's goalkicking percentage was the reason, everyone knew it was Cook's fall from grace that was behind the decision.'

Leading football journalist Mike Sheahan was asked about it in his 'Write to Mike' column in *The Herald Sun* in 2000.

Cook, he replied, was 'the face of the VFA for a long time'. 'Jim Miller was a great player and an excellent ambassador for the competition, but Cook's record would seem to be superior. Freddie's off-field indiscretions would not have helped his case.'

Ken Gannon was the head of Football Victoria (later AFL Victoria) when the medal was introduced. Gannon points out Miller won six goalkicking crowns and Cook five. Asked if Cook's law-breaking played a part in the decision, he laughs and says, 'Well, unless you were in the room you'll never know!'

It never bothered Cook that the medal was named after Miller, whom he respected as a player and a person. He called it a deserved accolade for a splendid career.

Dandy forward Pat Flaherty says that one word described both players: 'champion'.

Flaherty first played against Cook when he was at Yarraville and immediately thought him a 'sensational player'.

'He was a completely different player to Frosty,' Flaherty says. 'Frosty wasn't as big but he was a good lead and a great kick. He'd kick them from sixty or seventy metres out. But he was more unpredictable than Fred. He'd do the freakish thing, kick a freakish goal, and then he'd miss one from ten metres in front sort of thing. When I first started playing for Dandy, I remember Jimmy kicking 8.9 or 7.10, whereas I think Freddie was a bit more deadly. If Jimmy kicked straighter, he would have kicked a lot, lot more goals, especially early in his career. But everyone says the same about Fred.'

But in David 'Sam' Holt's mind, Cook had Miller covered. He believed Miller was a great player, but a great VFA player, the same as Joe Radojevic.

Cook, he thought, was in a different class. 'Fred was a VFL player who was playing in the VFA, and there was no better player in the VFA, by 100 yards, than Fred at his best,' Holt says. 'Let's not forget, he was at his best over a long period of time. We had some great players at Port, but I tell you what, we wouldn't have had the success if we didn't have him.'

Graham 'Buster' Harland agrees, calling Cook 'the best player who ever played VFA football'. 'He was a good mark, a shit kick, but he got the ball that many times it didn't make any difference,' he says.

ı|!ı

NORM Goss lost his long battle with cancer in March 1983. His funeral was said to be one of the largest in Port Melbourne.

His old mate Tommy Lahiff delivered a eulogy and penned a tribute for *The Emerald Hill and Sandridge Times*. 'I am not ashamed to say that as I write this, tears will not stop running from my eyes,' he wrote. 'If there is such a thing as love of one man for another, I am proud to say I loved Norman Leslie Goss.'

Shortly before his death, Goss had attended the annual VFA meeting. Marc Fiddian wrote that, when asked about his health, Goss told former Preston president Alex Robertson, 'If I can get through the summer I'll be all right. Port will pull me through the winter.'

'Goss quietly left his seat as 10.30pm approached,' Fiddian wrote. 'He looked a tired, forlorn figure as he walked towards the exit. Suddenly the whole assembly focused its attention on him and rose as one, applauding him for his fortitude. Goss half turned and acknowledged the warmth with a fleeting wave. The haggard Goss is not the one who will be remembered. Rather it is the vital, vigorous man who strode around the Port rooms in full control of everything before him.'

Cook says he wept for an hour when he heard Goss had died, believing he'd never meet another man his equal.

He says it was a privilege to share his company at the football club and the family home. Goss helped keep him in check, giving him firm advice and guidance throughout his career at Port Melbourne. Cook suspects an old-fashioned talking-to from 'Old Man Goss' might have set him right when he started taking drugs. He'd died by then. 'He wouldn't have been happy to see what I did post-Port,' Cook says. 'I know there's a lecture waiting for me.'

For a long time, Cook thought Port was never the same without its indefatigable administrator. It was as if the club had 'lost part of its soul'. He felt an emptiness every time he walked through the gate.

At the end of each season, Cook went to Goss to report that he had received big-money approaches from VFA, interstate, and country and suburban clubs, in the hope that he might bump up his match payment of $250 game.

One year, Dandenong made him a 'massive' offer as it sought to replace 'Frosty' Miller. 'Then you'd better start driving now — it's a long way to Dandenong,' Goss responded. When players coming off league lists put high price tags on their heads, Goss would scoff and say, 'Well, my top two wage earners here are Fred Cook and Stretch Aanensen — and you think you're better than them?'

Goss's long-time lieutenant, Charlie 'Dooley' Chrimes, recalls a

Port Melbourne–Williamstown match at North Port Oval. After it, Cook and a leading Willy official tapped at the door of the committee room, where Goss, Chrimes and Jack McFarlane were analysing the game.

Cook announced that Williamstown had offered him a bundle of money to transfer clubs. Goss didn't blink. 'Well, take it. You'll never get that sort of money here,' he said. About thirty minutes later, Cook reappeared on his own. 'Forget what I said earlier. I was only joking,' he said sheepishly.

Chrimes saw many other examples of Cook's impulsiveness. 'There was no tomorrow with Fred,' he says. 'It was all about today.'

He says Goss was a steadying influence on Cook, ensuring he trained and maintained his performances. When Goss died, he says, 'I don't think Fred had a shoulder to lean on, someone he could go to, to talk things through.'

In *A Different Breed*, Terry Keenan wrote that after Goss's death, Cook commissioned the portrait of him that takes pride of place in the Port Melbourne clubrooms. Cook has no memory of it. 'Geez, I can't remember that. But I'm glad I did. He deserved nothing less. It was only money to me back in those days.'

11

IT'S an apartment block now, at the corner of Station and Bridge streets in Port Melbourne. Three heavy black gates give access to the property.

What salacious stories this building could give up. Thirty years ago it operated as the Station Hotel — Fred Cook's Station Hotel, as large writing on the second storey trumpeted.

And when Cook ran it, it was one of the most frequented and talked-about watering holes in Melbourne. Legal figures, bankers, businessmen, police, entertainers and dozens of sporting identities were regular visitors.

The attraction was more than good food and cold beer. Cook employed topless waitresses and strippers, and bragged that his 'girls' were the most glamorous in Melbourne.

He would go to similar establishments, identify the most attractive performers and lure them to the Station with the offer of better money. One, former Penthouse model Christiana Jende, was so popular she regularly made more than $5000 a week. Cook liked to call her the perfect accompaniment to port and coffee.

Before taking over the Station Hotel, Cook had done well out of property.

He would buy a place, keep it for a couple of years and sell it for a tidy profit, starting with the house he picked up in Pitt Street, West Footscray with the Yarraville Football Club money. He sold it for more than double what he paid. From there he bought in Avondale Heights, Altona Meadows, South Melbourne and in Dendy Street, Brighton. He also had a three-level apartment at the prestigious Isle of Capri on the Gold Coast, complete with a rail line running to the edge of the Nerang River. Cook was also dabbling in bridging finance.

The Station Hotel was his biggest venture. Built in the 1850s, it had been reasonably successful in an area well off for hotels (Cook once counted nineteen in Port Melbourne, and thirty-three in South Melbourne and Albert Park).

But early in 1982, the operators disclosed to Bulletin magazine that they had been cashing 'ghost' tax refund cheques for the Painters and Dockers Union. The issue was raised at the Costigan Royal Commission into the union's activities.

Licensee Colin Johnston said he had been warned the hotel would be firebombed. There had earlier been hoax fire and ambulance calls, and threatening phone messages. A Painters and Dockers official was running an SP book on the premises, and Johnston had been forced to keep marijuana plants. Mr Costigan said Johnston's sister, Loris Cooper, was assaulted by a ship painter and docker.

'I have no hesitation in coming to the conclusion that members of the union have determined to drive Mrs Cooper out of business by threats of violence and actual violence,' Mr Costigan said.

Custom at the hotel dropped dramatically, the bank moved in and it was put on the market in September 1982.

The agent's listing said the 'freehold, land and buildings, licence and goodwill, furniture, plant and equipment' were to be auctioned.

The public bar, bistro/lounge, dining room, bottleshop, kitchen and public toilets were on the ground floor. Five bedrooms 'with the usual amenities' were upstairs.

'It was dead as a business at that stage,' Cook says. 'It had been black-banned. It was basically just sitting there.'

Cook, flanked by his mate Sam Newman, bid for the hotel up to $250,000, but was pipped. He was disappointed.

Cook was still working at Puma, but his association with the company was about to end over a large-scale theft of goods from the warehouse. Colleagues were staggered to learn of the allegations against him. He was interviewed at Russell Street Police Headquarters. Cook denied any involvement and was never charged. Still, he agreed to leave.

Two weeks after the auction of the hotel, the successful bidder contacted Cook and asked if he was interested in leasing it. He thought it an offer too good to refuse — no rent for the first month, then $1000 a week. The owner also promised a renovation, including new carpet, tables and chairs, an internal fire escape and sprinkler system, a remodeled kitchen, walk-in freezer and stainless steel lines for the beer.

A few months into life as a publican (he followed a line of footballers to get into the beer-pulling game, including his old teammate Dempsey, who had a pub in North Melbourne) he was offered the freehold of the Station. He agreed to buy it, but there was a problem with stamp duty and the sale never proceeded.

Cook installed as manager his non-drinking, non-smoking, bespectacled brother Rodney, who learned the business with one-week stints at other hotels, including under Brian 'Whale' Roberts at his premises in Clarendon Street, South Melbourne.

The four bars that had been empty began to fill from the day Cook moved in. His popularity as the champion Port Melbourne footballer was helping him empty his barrels of beer. The public bar had corrugated-iron walls and green carpet to make it look like an old football changing shed. Often it was so packed that drinkers stood shoulder to shoulder. Cook would stand behind the jump, pour drinks and chat to his patrons. He also brought in an experienced chef he knew only as 'Louie' (years later, people still vouch for his culinary skills, with Port Melbourne premiership player Buster Harland adamant he's never tasted a better marinara sauce).

'I was hand-ons. I had to be,' Cook says. 'As my old man said to me, "A lot of them have come just to see you." So I'd serve a few beers, and if someone important came in I'd go around and have a drink with them.'

His former Port Melbourne teammate Brendan Behan often dropped in to catch up with Cook and have a meal. 'Fred went into it with high expectations, which was fair enough because he was a celebrity in the town,' Behan says. 'There was another hotel called the Albion, where all the business people went. Fred thought he could up the ante. And he did. When it first opened, you couldn't get in. It was extraordinarily successful.'

He remembers that, under Cook's watch, the Station was turned into a stylish hotel equipped to cater for Port Melbourne's changing population. The gentrification of the working-class suburb was underway. It was becoming 'trendified', Behan remembers, with long-time residents selling up and starting-out couples moving in.

Joke-cracking Melbourne entertainer Maurie Fields played a black baby grand piano, comedienne and presenter Mary Hardy sang a few tunes, and singer Darryl Cotton's Fawlty Flowers, in nearby Bay

Street, delivered flowers daily.

Sam Newman says the lunches were 'legendary', attracting business leaders, politicians, law figures, police, entertainers and sportsmen. 'People wanted to be in Fred's company and at his gigs, and enjoy the revelry and merriment he afforded then. There was an absolute cross-section of society that would clamour to come to them,' he says, recalling the sight of a fleet of luxury cars parked outside the hotel.

He says interstate football supporters coming to Melbourne for a long weekend had two destinations: lunch at the Station Hotel on a Friday and a match on a Saturday. Members of the New Zealand cricket team also dropped in during their tour of Australia in 1985 to 1986.

Barman Doug Martinovic says the atmosphere was 'magic' and the hotel 'smartly run'.

Playing up his association with Port Melbourne, Cook went to *The Herald*, got photographs of past and present Borough players and coaches, and put them on the walls of the public bar.

Then he did something more risqué, employing a topless waitress in the upstairs meal area, which seated about thirty-five people.

He hired a university student — and he quickly needed to hire other women. It was a simple business decision, he says. He wanted to fill seats in a quieter part of the hotel.

'It caught on very quickly, just snowballed really,' Cook says. 'They were coming from everywhere.'

Loosening their ties and removing their jackets, businessmen were Cook's bread and butter. 'They felt they could come in and enjoy themselves among other business types and not feel like they were at a sleazy bloody strip joint,' he says. 'We were on a winner. We were kicking goals. Anybody who was anybody was dropping in.'

Strippers followed. Cook recalls, 'I said to one girl, "Love, can you dance?" Of course she could. So after you'd finished your meal, the sheila serving you with her tits hanging out would come back and get her gear off. We lifted the prices of the meals a bit upstairs — you paid $15 for an eye fillet or porterhouse served by the girls, but only $5 in the public bar — but I didn't hear one complaint. We promoted it as exclusive and expensive. They knew what they were in for.'

The combination of fine food and saucy sideshows created great demand for tables. Bookings were taken six weeks in advance, Cook says. In the end, he had to go downstairs. 'It was too big an opportunity to make money. The numbers spoke for themselves,' Cook says.

The hotel also began to host bucks' parties and birthdays.

'Best-looking women in town on show here,' Cook told his old opponent Phil Cleary when he turned up for a promotional photograph in 1984.

'It was true,' Cook says. 'They were fine-looking ladies. I actually got threatened by the other joints for stealing their best sheilas.'

'Private shows' were also available upstairs. One high-up Victorian legal figure often settled in for a show, emerging shirtless and with his chest glistening with baby oil.

Sports writer Scot Palmer and other scribes were regulars of the upstairs lunches. Palmer remembers the occasion when Jende removed Victorian Builders Labourers Federation boss Norm Gallagher's tie and rubbed it against her crotch. Someone suggested the tie should be raffled. 'You're not doing that — I'm taking it home,' Gallagher snorted.

'A lot of funny stuff like that went on. They were terrific days,' Palmer says. 'Fred was a great mine host, always buying drinks and keeping his customers happy. It was a beautiful old pub.'

At one point, rumours got around that Cook was running 'a knock-shop' at the hotel. He insists it was untrue. In 1985, police charged him with living off the earnings of prostitution, but he says he merely rang an escort agency on behalf of a patron. The patron happened to be an undercover police officer.

'I didn't need to live off the earnings of a prostitute,' Cook says. 'I was making more than enough. At our peak we were making $11,000 a week. Not $1100; $11,000. So why would I need a little sling from an escort agency?'

Behan, a lawyer, represented him in court (he was given a $500 good behaviour bond). He never understood why Cook turned the Station Hotel from an immensely popular and profitable business into what he regarded as a sleaze pit. 'Once he moved into the grey area, for want of a better expression, I stopped frequenting the place,' Behan says. 'There was no way known I was going to step back in there. It wasn't politic. I could never work out what caused him to move from legitimacy to quasi-legitimacy to illegitimacy.'

'I wanted a winner, something a bit more than just the food and the beer,' Cook responds. 'I wanted instant success, to strike while I was hot.'

The money was plentiful for Cook, but the hours were punishing. The hotel would open at 10am and close at midnight. He would oversee the cleaning up and generally go to bed at 2am. Four or five hours later he would be up to meet food suppliers for the kitchen. Cook was too busy making money to worry about a lack of sleep. But it contributed to him missing Port Melbourne training sessions. He was taking his eyes off the ball.

ı|||ı

THERE is one opponent no athlete can conquer: time. It stakes a claim on all of them. It happens to the best and it happens to the rest.

As he chased a fourth consecutive flag at Port Melbourne in 1983, Gary Brice saw that Fred Cook was slowing up. He was still a handful for the best backmen and still good for goals, but it was clear that age was catching up with the full forward.

Skipping training, his fitness declined and it was rare to see him use his pace and lead for the ball, preferring to battle for marks from the goal square. Brice agonised over it, but decided to drop him late in the season. Cook gained a reprieve when big Brett Chadband pulled out of the senior side with injury.

He was named in the ruck. 'What?' he asked, incredulous when Brice told him where he would be playing. The coach said the selectors had no other choice since he was the only senior player over six foot two who was fit and available. Brice also told Cook it appeared his career was coming to a close. 'I'll play until I'm forty,' Cook snapped. 'That's fine,' Brice answered, 'but it won't be here.'

Brice remembers Cook doing well in the ruck. 'He actually played a couple of blinders,' he says.

Despite his diminishing returns, Cook finished the season with seventy-six goals. Teammate Graeme Anderson broke his long run as the Borough's leading goalkicker, nailing ninety-two.

Anderson, an opportunist forward good enough to play seventy-one games for Collingwood, remembers that Cook spilled a lot of marks that season.

'He dropped more than what he used to,' he says. 'I've told a lot of people this: he still outpointed whoever was on him and got his hands first to the ball, but in 1983 they didn't stick like they normally did.'

Port, having defeated Sandringham in the first semi-final, was humbled by Geelong West in the preliminary final. Cook did most of the ruck work, but still contributed four of the Borough's six goals. Brice said it was an excellent performance from Cook and a worthy effort from his team, considering injuries cut so deep during the year.

Glen Robertson won the best and fairest. But Swan won his second J. J. Liston Trophy, cementing his standing as a Port Melbourne champion.

Brice resigned at the end of the season, joining Essendon as a skills coach under Kevin Sheedy. He was content at the Bombers, but Jack 'Darkie' McFarlane, another fine and long-serving Port administrator, enticed him back to the Borough for the 1985 season. By that time, Fred Cook had moved on.

12

FRED Cook had told Gary Brice he wanted to play for Port Melbourne until he was forty. In fact, he wanted to play forever.

Football had given him a large public profile and the popularity that he turned into success off the ground. It was his business to kick goals. They were behind the properties and the money and the adulation.

There was pressure to perform. 'How many will you kick today, Fred?' star-eyed youngsters would ask as he walked through the gates.

But Cook enjoyed playing the game. Taking a big mark or snapping a goal from the boundary gave him a sensation he couldn't experience the other six days of the week. He called it the 'buzz in the belly'. It had been like that ever since he started playing as a schoolboy. Even if he didn't have above-average ability, he says, he would have played suburban football for a long time.

But in 1984, his Port Melbourne career was coming to an end. And he had no say in it. It was out of his hands, the hands that had served him so well in the VFA for fifteen years.

Former Fitzroy and Collingwood star Warwick Irwin had replaced Brice as coach. From the outset he encountered problems with Cook. He was late to training, if he arrived at all, and his performances were patchy.

When he was playing league football (well enough to win Fitzroy's best and fairest in 1975) Irwin watched the VFA 'religiously' and regarded Port's full forward as 'an absolute legend'. He thought him an 'enormous talent'.

'When I say "legend", I'm talking about not only at Port, but in the VFA community,' Irwin says. 'I used to watch the VFA just to watch him. A lot of people did.'

But that was then. Snowed under at the Station Hotel, and with his various media commitments and sportsman's nights, Cook would ring Irwin and tell him he couldn't get to training, something that would never have happened under the watch of Norm Goss. Irwin heard lots of excuses.

One night, Cook said his car had broken down outside the pub. Irwin remembers the conversation going like this:

Cook: 'It's in pieces on the nature strip.'

Irwin: 'Well, what do you know about cars?'

Cook: 'I don't know anything about 'em.'

Irwin: 'Okay. Fair enough. But why can't you come to training?'

Cook: 'Didn't you hear me? I told you the car's in pieces.'

Irwin: 'Fred, the pub's only 400 metres from the ground. Have you ever thought of walking or, even better, jogging here?'

Cook: 'Cut it out mate, I've got an image to live up to in this town.'

Irwin recalls Cook phoning him to say a water bed at the hotel was leaking. Irwin says, 'I said, "So, what's the issue? How will that stop you training?" And he said, "The water is flooding through the ceiling and onto the customers in the bar."'

Cook was having to earn his goals like never before. He began to panic if he didn't have any by quarter time. It was why he used to tell supremely talented Port youngster Jason Love, who Irwin had introduced to the senior team, to 'help get me on the board early, young fella'.

In Round 7 he yanked back the clock, torching Frankston for ten goals. He hurt his right arm at the start of the third quarter, had it strapped, kept playing and booted six in the second half.

Love remembers that Cook 'hardly trained' in 1984 and would turn up fifteen minutes before games in a suit and make-up, having come straight from the set of *World of Sport*, where he was doing the VFA segment. Love grew up watching Cook and counted him as a hero. He went on to play league football. But he regards sharing the forward line with 'big Freddie' as a highlight of his time in football. 'He was like a rock star,' Love says. 'He was as big as anything in the game back then.'

Early in the season, Irwin had a reminder of Cook's stature in the competition.

'Come on mate, how about you give me a fair go today,' Cook said to the umpire in the Port rooms before the match. The umpire replied: 'The first time the ball goes down there I'll look after you. After that, you're on your own.'

'Well bugger me dead, the first time it went into our forward line Cookie wasn't within ten metres of the action,' Irwin says. 'But, *bip*, the umpire blows the whistle and gives him a free kick! I heard what he'd said to Cookie, but I didn't think it would happen. Bloody oath it happened!'

But Irwin's patience was wearing and he gave Cook three or four warnings to 'get your act together'.

Finally, after Cook played poorly in a loss to Preston as the Borough laboured to stay in finals contention (they ended up missing the final four for the first time in twelve years), Irwin resolved to act.

He knew it was a momentous decision to dump such a Port Melbourne icon. But he also knew no player was bigger than the club, not even Fabulous Fred Cook.

He decided to tell him at selection (Cook was on the match committee) that he had to retire. Irwin had the support of others at the meeting.

Irwin recalls, 'I just came out and said, "Well, Cookie's not in my team." And Cookie said, "Well, he's in my team!" I looked down at the other blokes and they said, "Nah, he's not in our team either." I turned to him and said, "Cookie, this is it, mate." He asked me what I meant. I said that unfortunately his time had come, it was all over. I said he'd made an enormous contribution to Port Melbourne and the VFA, but this is what it had come to. Fred said, "I'll play in the seconds." I told him he wouldn't be playing in the bloody seconds. He said, "Why not?" I said I wouldn't do that to him. We had to convince him.'

Cook was taken aback. He wasn't ready to be a relic. He argued his case for retention in the team and said he would make a greater effort to train. But the match committee members were unmoved. Cook finally accepted that Port Melbourne, the club for which he had kicked 1236 goals (winning eleven goalkicking awards), played a record 253 games and featured in six premierships, no longer wanted him.

He asked Irwin if he could tell the players he was retiring (Port had named him in the team to head off questions about his future). Cook delivered the news two days later at a Saturday morning training run. Irwin remembers that he spoke for a long time — and finished with a pop at the coach. Cook told the players that all the coaches he played under at the Borough had their photos on the wall of the Station Hotel. 'But this bastard,' he said, pointing to Irwin, 'his photo will never get there.'

'I thought it was fair enough,' Irwin says. 'I was happy to cop that because he was upset. He was really upset. He probably got away with things that other players wouldn't have got away with, because he'd built up a credit bank, if you like. But by that stage he was a shadow of his former self. Sad, really. I think running the Station Hotel took over his life and football was the loser. Cookie probably could have played another couple of years if he'd knuckled down.

'It was a bloody hard thing to do because everyone loved him. But when push came to shove, we were about winning games — and he wasn't helping us do that anymore. It's a funny thing. If blokes are playing well and the team is winning, clubs overlook their weaknesses. But when the team isn't winning the games it's expected to win, clubs start looking for why-aren't-wes. And as coach, I was looking for the why-aren't-wes. One was Fred Cook. He wasn't producing.'

Irwin says he was mindful that legends such as Cook deserved to go out on their own terms, and that he was tapping the shoulder of an iconic Port Melbourne and VFA player. 'Even though he probably thinks I never thought about that, I thought about it a lot. But it came down to the bottom line, winning games of football and clubs being greater than the individual.'

Although Cook is adamant that he hadn't touched drugs when he was at Port Melbourne, Irwin isn't so sure, remembering a game when Cook was in 'ga-ga land'. Irwin took him off the ground in the last quarter. After the match, two women appeared at his side and dragged him out of the changerooms. Cook said he was concussed and was going to see a doctor. He recovered quickly; that night it got back to Irwin that his veteran forward was doing the rounds of the nightclubs.

Port Melbourne defender Greg 'Biff' Dermott sympathised with

Irwin. He liked Cook, counted him a four-time premiership teammate and considered him an 'unbelievable' player and an 'icon' of the VFA.

But he watched with increasing frustration as Cook dodged training sessions. Dermott and other players became annoyed at his no-shows, thinking he was putting himself ahead of the team. At Port Melbourne, that was unacceptable.

'Warwick wanted a disciplined side and that was good. He was always up-front about that,' Dermott says. 'But Fred could do what he could without much work on the track. Everyone knows that. His training ability, when he wanted to do it, he was one of the best going around. He'd turn around and say, "I'm the quickest in the group." And we'd say, "Fred, how about we see it?" And he'd say, "Well, I don't have to do it all the time, I just do it when I want." You'd have a joke about it, and all of a sudden he'd just ping out of the blocks and beat everyone in the sprints. Warwick's view was that Fred had to produce it more or less all the time. He wanted a bit of discipline out of Fred. He had no chance.'

Dermott remembers Cook often arriving late for training, saying he'd been busy at the hotel. One Saturday morning he turned up after a lot of drink and little sleep — and was barely able to run.

Dermott has never forgotten how, before his debut against Dandenong at Shepley Oval, Cook told him he was responsible for his selection.

'He said, "I pushed you up for a game." I was wet behind the ears, and said, "Oh, thanks for that, Fred." When I thought about it later it made me realise Fred always wanted to be the main man, the limelight sort of guy.'

Cook went along with the club's line that he had chosen to retire because of business pressures. He didn't want Port Melbourne to receive any criticism over his departure, believing better men than him had taken the tap on the shoulder.

He told *Sun* reporter Michael Reid he'd had a 'good innings' and he had to 'weigh up my own contribution to the team rather than go on an individual ego trip'. The newspaper splashed a photograph of him on the back page, boots in one hand and drink in the other as he stood at the bar of his hotel. It was, *The Sun* said, the 'end of an era'.

A statement released by the club said Cook had found it 'increasingly difficult to dedicate himself to training and to performing to the standards he would expect of himself and expected by the club'.

But Cook says now that he didn't retire. He was sacked.

He had kicked sixty-one goals in 1984, five more than Love, and felt he had been playing reasonably well. Although there had been warnings to 'smarten up', he was shocked at what unfolded at the match committee meeting.

The finality of it hit him like a bus. He had always imagined his career ending with an armchair ride off the ground, waving his thank-yous to the Borough supporters who so adored him. Maybe he could even go out on the high of another premiership. But there would be nothing like that, no farewell match, no good-byes. He had played his last game.

'Didn't see it coming. No, not at all. If they were going to drop me, I wanted to play in the seconds, help the kids out,' he says. 'No shame in that. Bob Bonnett did that after he finished up in the seniors, went back and played in the seconds. But I think Henry Harrison [Port's president at the time] thought the committee would get lynched by the supporters if I was dropped to the seconds.'

Thirty years later, he still rolls the numbers through his head and weighs them to his advantage.

'They chucked me out with four matches to go. So if we made the finals there's another two matches … I could have almost kicked 100 goals playing badly! Christ, if a young kid had done what I did that year they would have given him a major award at the end of the season!

'But now I can understand why they did it. I wasn't approaching football like I always had. It slipped down the list of my priorities. Football had always been my first concern. In 1984 it wasn't.

'It was a bitter pill to swallow, to be given the flick. I'd been playing football since I was twelve. It was my life, my whole regime, really. Then, bang, see you later.'

Charlie 'Dooley' Chrimes was saddened to see the departure of a player he helped recruit fourteen years earlier. But, noting Cook's thinning returns and waning commitment, he thought Irwin and the club had made the right decision. Chrimes puts the full forward in the same class as Borough ruck great Frank Johnson, 'only because Fred won us premierships'. 'His performances in grand finals were unbelievable,' Chrimes says.

Told his days were done, Cook went back to the Station Hotel and cried, eldest daughter Jacqueline at his side. He likened the end of his career to a train operating under full steam coming to a grinding halt. He was 'shattered'.

'It hit me harder than what I ever let on,' he says. 'Just to talk about it now has my mind spinning around. Yeah. Fuck, it hurt.'

He remembers getting drunk that night. But that had become common. Always fond of beer, he would pour himself a pot as he worked behind the bar and drink steadily during the day. He saw the bottom of countless glasses. By 1985, when he was regularly taking amphetamines, he had switched to Bacardi and Coke, and would often guzzle a litre a day and stay sober. It was like lolly water to him.

In the VFA Record, two Port Melbourne businesses — Shield's Transport and Bay Street Meats — took out advertising congratulating Cook on his career.

In *The Emerald Hill and Sandridge Times*, Tom Lahiff paid a handsome tribute to the Borough No. 5. Cook had been 'hit with everything that could be thrown at him', but 'answered all their attacks on the scoreboard', Lahiff wrote.

'Fred had a very strong pair of hands and once they touched the ball, it was his. I've always been critical of his kicking and if he'd been accurate he would have kicked 2000 goals ... but Fred, all is forgiven.

'Port Melbourne, the VFA and the kids are going to miss this great personality. He has been a drawcard and credit to the game and it will be a big loss. I always have sad feelings when players such as Fred Cook come to the end of the line. I wish they could go on forever, but time catches up with everyone.'

He concluded by calling him a champion.

Cook's first marriage was also over. For years he was unfaithful to Bernadette, who his Port Melbourne teammates remember as an excellent mother and a decent, kind woman true to her Catholic upbringing.

Other women, many attracted by his standing in football, had availed themselves to Cook and he couldn't resist. When opportunities didn't present, he went looking. He never saw a pretty lady he didn't fancy. 'Fred was like a heat-seeking missile,' lawyer Bernie Balmer says.

Cook maintained relationships outside his marriage. One produced a child, Robert Rapkin. The family fold could never hold him.

'She [Bernadette] put up with a lot, much more than she should have. I regret it, very much so. It caused a lot of hurt to the people closest to me,' Cook says.

He falls into sheepishness when discussing his first marriage, acknowledging a lack of respect for a woman with whom he has not spoken for thirty years. 'I'm not proud of what happened. Bernadette was a good woman, a fine woman. I couldn't see what I had, didn't realise how lucky I was. I was always about the now.'

The 'now' meant he had numerous female partners. A former member of a Port Melbourne match committee shakes his head as he remembers the night an anxious Cook asked him when the selection meeting would be finishing. Soon, the committeeman replied, 'Why, what's the rush, Fred?' Cook explained he had arranged to meet one woman at a flat at 8pm, another at 9.30pm and a third lady at the Chevron Hotel at midnight. More than one Port teammate wondered how he had the energy to kick his goals after hearing him boast about his sexual activities.

There were flings with a popular Australian television actress, the daughters of two politicians of international standing, and a string of models. Many people have heard the names, because Cook has never been shy about discussing his conquests.

Most commonly, he talks about the time he was intimate with the secretary of a Liberal Party MP. The encounter ended with Cook tracing her bottom on blotting paper on the politician's desk and writing him a message. He phoned Cook the next day to say he was not amused. Cook apologised — then said it had been quite the experience.

The story about the video he inadvertently slipped to Sam Newman did the rounds of Melbourne years ago.

Newman was a ruck coach at Footscray and had under his wing Andrew Purser, a brilliant big man from WA. He took the tape of a Bulldogs game to Cook, asking him to cut it down to the ruck highlights. Newman collected the edited copy and sat down with Purser at his home to talk through his performance and dispense a few tips.

Purser's parents had come over from the west. Along with his wife, Jenny, they were in the lounge room sipping tea when Newman hit play. 'The cassette's in and I'm pointing out to Andrew what he's doing well,' Newman says. 'Then it went blank and the half time siren went, and it came on again.

'Now, I'm not sure if Fred did this on purpose, but the first thing back after half time was Fred having sexual relations with two girls. I looked at it and Andrew's parents looked at it. I had my leg in plaster and my hand in plaster at the time. But I sprang off my good leg and I headbutted the cassette machine out of the cabinet. I was on the floor and I looked back to see Mrs Purser. She had got the tea to her lips and she had frozen. And that is absolute gospel.'

His former sister-in-law, Kim McNamara, describes Cook's relations with women in unvarnished terms: 'Fred couldn't keep his dick in his pants. He was bloody hopeless. He loved women madly. But he loved them all.'

Cook says he had 'far more opportunities' than many other men and he rarely let them pass. 'When you've got pretty women wanting to get with you, it's exciting, it fans your ego. I'd get with them as quick as you could pull one from under me. Geez, I would.'

But he acknowledges he hurt quite a few with promises of relationships he had no intention of pursuing. It was the 'gift of the gab'. He always had it. 'But a lot of the time they took me on face value. There were a few broken hearts along the way. I'm putting my hand up for that.'

Former Borough player Brendan Behan calls Cook a 'likeable,

generous, big-hearted person who clearly had a weakness where it came to the other sex'. 'But it wasn't for me to sit in judgement of him. And he wasn't on his Pat Malone in that regard,' Behan says.

His third wife, Sally Desmond, says Cook grew up in a culture in which footballers strove to be 'players' off the field as well as on it. The fact that he enjoyed a level of fame brought women to his door, she says. They were eager to have their 'five minutes of fame' with a well-known footballer.

'They knew damn well he was married, but it didn't stop them,' Desmond says. 'They wanted to get a notch in their belts.'

Cook cheated on Desmond 'too many times to count'.

'He shattered my heart a few times. But what do you do? You can pack up and leave. But I didn't. I stayed. So I was just as silly,' she says. 'But when you love someone, you stay. I come from a line of long marriages in my family. My grandparents were married 61-and-a-half years. My parents have now been married sixty-two years. Fred was the father of my children, so of course I wanted to make it work. You don't just give up on someone because ... okay, the tarting around was pretty shattering ... but once I'd made a commitment I stuck to it, for all his bad habits. I gave it my best shot, anyway.'

Her solicitor once told her he had never seen a more loyal person.

13

JUST as a criminal element had attached itself to the hotel under the previous owners, some of Fred Cook's regulars were well known to police. As he says, a few had seen more stations than Puffing Billy.

But because of his stature as a great Port Melbourne footballer, he encountered no trouble in his early days at the hotel. The only time he saw a punch thrown was when a suspicious wife found her husband having lunch with his secretary upstairs. There was no drug dealing, no prostitution, no gambling, no violence.

In 1984, Cook was introduced to a heavily tattooed man named 'Dennis'. He was wearing green brace and bib overalls and white running shoes, drinking Southern Comfort and Coke, and chain-smoking Viscounts at the bar. Cook saw that he liked to wear expensive jewellery — lots of it. He thought Dennis was a blowhard, but he let it go because he was spending a lot of money, tipping big and shouting drinks to people around him.

To his great regret, Cook got to know Dennis too well.

Dennis was Dennis Allen, and he was one of Melbourne's most violent criminals. A lot has been written about him since his death in 1987 and he's invariably described as a 'notorious' underworld figure.

In the 1980s, he lived in Richmond and made a fortune selling drugs and firearms. At one stage he had converted his heroin dealing into nine properties in the suburb.

It was unwise to mess with him. Some who did never lived to regret it. A body count piled up around him. Allen was suspected of, but never charged with, a string of murders.

Allen was the first child of Kath Pettingill. Two of her other sons, Victor Peirce and Trevor Pettingill, were two of the men charged over the murders of Victorian police officers Steven Tynan (aged twenty-two) and Damian Eyre (aged twenty) in Walsh Street, South Yarra, in 1988.

The slaying of the young constables was said to be a payback for the death of Melbourne criminal Graeme Jensen a few days earlier. Jensen had been shot by police in his car as they tried to arrest him at Narre Warren.

The four men charged in connection with Walsh Street were acquitted. After the case, Kath Pettingill sheeted home the blame to Allen.

'We're still paying for his sins,' she told television reporter Martin King. 'We all are. He died before he could be punished.'

In his classic crime book *Untold Violence*, Melbourne writer Tom Noble described Allen as a 'small-time criminal who made good'. 'He knew some of the best criminals in Melbourne and many of the city's leading detectives. As a violent drug dealer who amassed a sizeable personal fortune, he also killed, more than once.'

Tony Farrell, whose son Anthony was one of the men charged over the Walsh Street murders, often drank at the Station Hotel. He introduced Cook to Allen.

Cook approached him as he did all his customers, chatting and making sure his glass was filled and he was comfortable in his surrounds. Allen was; he became a regular. He had watched Cook play for Port Melbourne and often asked him about his career. Cook was happy to talk football and whatever else Allen wanted to yarn about. After all, he would often spend $1000 in one sitting, on drinks, meals and tips.

Eventually, Cook came to understand that his cashed-up patron acquired his money in a way less lawful than what he did.

'He just opened up and said he was selling heroin and he was making shitloads of money out of it,' Cook says. 'I mean, shitloads, ridiculous amounts.'

Sports writer Scot Palmer knew all about Dennis Allen. In the early 1980s, Palmer and his family took over the Cherry Tree Hotel in Richmond, not far from where Allen had bought his string of properties.

Allen spent a lot of time at the Cherry Tree, considering it his 'local' and his turf. But Palmer was out to run a successful hotel and was intent on stamping out its criminal crowd. Allen quickly came to dislike him. He would pay for his Southern Comfort and Coke with $50 notes and leave the change. But the Palmers, not wanting to be 'bought', always set it aside and handed it back when he next visited.

More than once, bullets were fired into the walls of the hotel.

Palmer and his wife, Lorraine, lived on their nerves. They were 'constantly on alert, wondering who would be next through the door and would there be a confrontation', he wrote in *The Sunday Herald Sun* in 1996. 'Whenever it was Dennis and his spiky-haired nephew Jason Ryan, in their identical work overalls and snow-white sandshoes with the lace holes removed, our hearts sank.'

Palmer banned Allen after a nose-to-nose argument and was later told a contract had been placed on his life.

Later still, an Allen henchman pulled a pistol on him and former TV crooner Terry Holden, threatening to blow away their testicles. Palmer's son, Lincoln, in turn pointed his hunting rifle at the hood, heading off gun fire.

Warwick Irwin, Port Melbourne's coach in 1984, felt the end of Allen's temper during the season. Borough players and their wives and partners were having a private dinner at the Station. Irwin was about to start eating his meal when Cook pulled him aside and said, 'There's a bloke at the front door who wants to join us.' Who was he? Irwin asked. Was he a player or a committeeman? Cook said no. 'Well, tell him he can't come in,' Irwin replied. Cook said he couldn't do that because 'he's a local and they might black ban the hotel'.

Irwin rose from his seat and said he would tell the fellow he was unwelcome. 'I fronted the bloke and he said he barracked for the Borough. I said that was fantastic, but he could come in for a drink next time we were playing a home game,' Irwin recalls. 'He wouldn't have a bar of it. He wanted to knock me out, he wanted to do all sorts of bloody things to me. The guy happened to be Dennis Allen. I won't go any further, but there was a gun involved. Seriously.'

That year, Allen invited Cook to his house in Stephenson Street, Richmond. Geese wandered around the backyard. Allen explained they guarded property better than dogs.

But Cook remembers the visit more for gunfire than the waterfowl.

They were sitting in the lounge room when Allen walked out and returned with a Magnum Highway Patrolman.

'He said, "Them fuckin' coppers are up on the bell tower [the Bryant and May factory across the road]." And he's gone *ping, ping, ping*, shooting at them,' Cook says. 'I just couldn't believe it. He's taking pot shots at the cops who were doing surveillance on him.'

Cook was startled. But it didn't stop him from going around there again two weeks later. He shared a Southern Comfort and Coke with Allen, listened to Bob Marley music, admired the exotic fish swimming in giant tanks and snorted cocaine. The affable former Port Melbourne football champion was keeping bad company and getting into bad habits.

ı|lı

'HERE,' Dennis Allen said, taking Fred Cook's drink, a Bacardi and Coke. 'Try this.'

Allen pulled a bag of white powder from his trouser pocket, put some on a pen knife and tipped it into Cook's drink. Standing behind the bar of his Station Hotel, Cook drank it in one pull and quickly felt a lot better.

Cook had been battling the flu, and on this day late in 1984 he was feeling lousy. He was down to do a sportsman's night at a suburban football club with St Kilda's Brownlow Medal star Neil Roberts and English Test cricketer John Snow, and needed to be at his sharpest to tell his football stories and raise a few laughs.

He explained his plight to Allen, who said he had just the answer, reaching for the bag. It was the first time Cook had taken speed. Straight away he got a tremendous lift. 'I felt bloody fantastic,' he says.

He began to use it more regularly, figuring he had it worked out. It was simple maths: if he took twice as much he'd feel twice as good.

Cook was developing a habit when he decided, at age thirty-seven, to continue his VFA career in 1985.

His Port Melbourne premiership teammate David 'Sam' Holt was coaching Second Division club Moorabbin. Cook always admired

Holt — he thought him classy and courageous, and believed he should have captained the Borough — and he phoned him and asked if he needed a full forward. Did he what!

Trouble was, Holt told Cook, the club, rebuilding after years out of the competition, had no money. There was no way Moorabbin could afford him. That was fine, Cook replied. He'd play for nothing. He told Moorabbin officials he only wanted a roll of beer tickets after games so he could shout drinks to friends who came to watch him. Sam Newman often dropped in.

Moorabbin official Bruce Whalebone was predicting the club's recruit would kick 100 goals 'if our players learn how to deliver the ball to him'.

In an article in *The Sunday Press*, Cook said he wanted to put something back into the game. He said Moorabbin was a young side and 'should benefit by having an old bloke with a bit of experience at full forward'.

Cook lined up in the last practice match against Mordialloc. Through the concertina doors separating the changerooms, Holt heard Mordi backman Mark Sarau say he wanted to pick up Cook. 'I think Fred kicked six on him just in the first quarter,' Holt recalls. 'He won our boys over straight away.'

A week later he jagged ten goals against Dandenong in Round 1. Moorabbin missed the four only on percentage and Cook booted seventy-two goals, fifth on the table (Oakleigh champion Rino Pretto led the count with an astonishing 170).

Cook says he enjoyed his time at Moorabbin and still relished 'sticking it up some full back'. But his drug use had escalated to the point where he would sometimes sneak into the toilets at half time and inject himself. He called it a 'plug'.

However, Cook is adamant the amphetamines detracted from his performance. 'What happens is, you can't focus on one thing. You start 100 things and don't finish one of them. When you're playing football, you need to be able to concentrate on what's happening in front of you. So when your brain is all over the place it's not really helping you. It's like an overload of electricity shooting around your head. Nah, you can't play good footy when that's zapping through you.'

Bob Profitt, who played in Port Melbourne's 1976 and 1977 premierships, was playing in the bush in 1985 but training at Moorabbin under Holt (they were best men at each other's weddings).

Running around the streets of Moorabbin one night, Profitt passed on a rumour he'd heard: that Fred Cook was on drugs. 'Sam stopped in his tracks,' Profitt remembers. 'He was shocked.'

Confirmation came eight weeks into the season, when one of Cook's relatives phoned Holt. It did explain some of Cook's behaviour. Holt noticed he talked at '100 miles an hour' and could be moody.

'I wanted to sack him at one stage there,' Holt says. 'I pulled him up in the rooms. He hadn't had a kick for a couple of weeks. I said, "Just retire, give it away." He said he didn't want to. He got emotional. He said, "Give me one more week, can you please give me one more week?" The next day I got told from someone close to him that he'd been doing drugs for a fair while. That's when the penny dropped.

'He was terrific early doors. He was training and having a go, and he was really good with the young players. But he slowly went backwards. He could still clunk it — and you wouldn't find a better mark of a football — but there were days when he just wouldn't touch it. That was probably because of the stuff he was taking.'

Holt suspected Cook went to Moorabbin to become the first VFA player to reach 300 games.

It came at Waverley and the VFA Record gave a suitable splash to the 'popular VFA innkeeper'. Holt says the day 'turned into a bit of a circus'. In the lead-up to the match he asked Cook if there was anything planned for the milestone. 'Not that I know of,' he replied. But TV cameras turned up and took over the rooms, crowding the players as they did their warm-ups.

'It was a distraction,' Holt says. 'But looking back, the players probably enjoyed that day. They really liked Fred. He always had stories. He was a poor man's E. J. Whitten in a way, always pumping up life. He was good for the club. He created a lot of interest in Moorabbin, same as he did at Port and for the VFA. I mean, he was the VFA in the 1970s. He dragged people through the gates.'

Steve Barnes, who was coaching Waverley, says it was a big occasion for the club. He remembers his young defender Andrew Fisher keeping Cook under control and helping the Panthers to a close victory.

After the match, Waverley president Frank Buck made a presentation to Cook. Then the party began. Cook hung around as the band The Drifters performed in the social club. 'No-one worked Monday — oh for the old job at Telecom,' Barnes says.

Graham Stewart, who captained Moorabbin in 1985, recalls Cook's season as much for his well-kept appearance as his goalkicking. He says his high-profile teammate took two bags to games — one for his football gear and the other for his hair dryer and deodorants. 'He used to look a million dollars when he ran onto the ground,' Stewart says. 'Geez, he was a funny bastard, Fred. Such a great bloke. He used to take us to the pub and really look after us.'

He's always remembered how Cook told him he disliked playing at Oakleigh. He thought it 'a prick of a joint' because it had no power points for his hair dryer.

Cook exited the VFA not with a bang, but blowing bubbles. The last of his eighteen games for Moorabbin was against Brunswick and umpired by Frank Vergona.

A small man who hitched his white shorts high, Vergona was the best-known whistleblower in the VFA in the 1970s and 1980s, and handled Port Melbourne's 1980 and 1982 grand finals. He knew Cook well, right back to his stint at Yarraville, when he saw him dominate a match against Geelong West as a ruck rover. Vergona umpired numerous matches involving Cook, and regarded him as the best and fairest player in the VFA.

It so happened that on this day in 1985, he walked through the gate with him. He remembers thinking, *Gee, Fred, you look a bit worse for wear*. 'I'd heard things weren't going too well in his life at that stage,' Vergona says. 'I thought, *God, look after yourself, Fred, because things might not turn out too well*.'

Before a crowd recorded in *The Sun* as 500 people, Cook booted one goal in a 25-point victory. It was a modest sign-off from a competition in which he played for seventeen seasons, the bulk of them as its most bewitching, brilliant figure.

Vergona says it was a shame a player he'd seen kick hundreds of goals went out so quietly. 'He was an incredible player, an incredible drawcard. I used to love umpiring Fred Cook. Swanny [Billy Swan] would stream out of the centre and look for him, and he knew where to run. He was virtually unstoppable. Oh God, what great days.'

ı|lı

WITH a grey-suited Sam Newman acting as best man, Cook was married again, to Port Melbourne girl Karen McNamara, in 1985.

They had been seeing each other for about eight years, long enough for them to buy a house together in Iffla Street, South Melbourne (number 96, and it shared certain characteristics of the saucy Australian television drama *Number 96*). Friends remember it as a tempestuous relationship.

McNamara, ten years his junior, was fiercely protective of him — she once gave Port Melbourne coach Gary Brice a mouthful for playing her man in the ruck — and did her best to stop his drug use. Cook would hide his amphetamines in any place in the hotel he thought she wouldn't find it: under the bed, in coverings for the fire alarm, in pots and pans in the kitchen.

But the strong-willed McNamara would uncover his stash and get rid of the drugs. It led to blazing arguments. 'We had so many blues about it,' he says. 'It's a "now" drug, and if I wanted it now and she'd turfed it, I'd be pretty pissed off.'

When he felt like a plug, he would lie to get out of the hotel. He'd say he had to drop in to the bank or fill up with petrol or visit a football pal or a family member.

'When I got to the car I'd drive 100 miles an hour to get to my supplier,' he says. 'That's all I gave a shit about, putting a fit [needle] in my arm.'

It took planning. If he was out of speed he'd have to phone his dealer to arrange a pick-up. He had to make sure he had a clean needle. He had to peel away from people and find a quite place to inject. 'When everything was right, I'd be very happy, relaxed,' he says. 'I could go for it.'

His marriage to McNamara failed to see out twelve months. That was no surprise to many people. There were constant rows before and after the exchange of vows at a Uniting Church in Dorcas Street,

South Melbourne on a Monday afternoon.

On one occasion, Cook flung open the door of the Golden Gate Hotel in South Melbourne and walked in with a woman on each arm. The McNamara sisters just happened to be at the hotel. 'Fancy meeting you here!' he said. Karen splashed a drink over him.

She also caught him cheating at a Swanston Street townhouse after discovering his Ford LTD in the carpark. McNamara, hysterical, got in the car and ploughed through the boomgate. The box used to collect tokens at the exit ended up as collateral in the back seat.

In one incident, McNamara wound up in hospital after walking in on Cook and a young woman at the Station Hotel. A bottle of wine and glasses were thrown, and her hand was badly cut when it went through a window.

More than once, the hotel chef arrived at work to find that clothes had been scattered on the street after another row between the couple.

Cook sometimes told McNamara he had to head interstate for a sporting function. He would ring her and when she answered the phone he would play a tape recording of the STD pips of a long-distance call. When she eventually found out, he complimented her for being a 'good detective'. She needed no great sleuthing powers to work out that when he dropped red roses off at her workplace, he might have more flowers in the back of his car for other women. She was right. 'He was out doing the rounds for Valentine's Day,' McNamara says.

She despised Cook's drug-taking and the criminal company he was keeping. Returning to the hotel late one night, she discovered her bed occupied by Dennis Allen and his girlfriend. He pulled a gun, shot out the light and threatened her. McNamara, who describes herself as 'full of fire' and 'never backwards in coming forwards', wrestled the firearm off him, hid it and demanded he leave. Weeks later, Allen kidnapped her when she went to the Cherry Tree Hotel to visit Scot and Lorraine Palmer, ripping her top off, shooting holes in it and holding her captive in the Stephenson Street house. She escaped by plying him with alcohol and taking the keys when he finally passed out on the couch, a firearm dangling from his pocket.

McNamara suspected Allen had been adding heroin to the speed he supplied to Cook. She also suspected Cook was spiking her own drinks, to keep him company as he dodged sleep.

McNamara saw Cook changing before her eyes, turning from an affable and caring man into something more sinister. 'He even started talking like Dennis Allen,' she recalls. 'He changed so much. I was like, "What the hell is happening to you, what the fuck are you doing?" He became this monster.'

A Port Melbourne supporter, she had thought Cook a 'big head' when he emerged from the changerooms after matches with his hair blow-dried. She had no interest in him. But he chased her relentlessly and she fell for him, in particular his sense of humour. 'He just used to make me laugh so much,' she says. 'That's all we did in the early days, just laugh.'

But she found life with the football star was less glamorous than she imagined. Yes, she accompanied him to a lot of exclusive events. But she tired of the affairs — 'how many times can someone rip your heart out?' — the lies and the drugs.

Still, she went ahead with the wedding. 'Well, I was in love, madly crazy in love, and it does stupid things to you,' she says. 'At the end of the day, you always think he might change. But you couldn't change Fred. You know what they say: a leopard never changes its spots.'

Guests who attended the reception still laugh at the speeches. Sam Newman told how he penciled the date in his diary since there was every chance he would have to erase it.

The day after the wedding, Cook had a surprise for his new bride, saying he had agreed to take in Allen's fourteen-year-old nephew Jason Ryan (later the prosecution's star witness in the Walsh Street murder case).

They drove to court for a hearing, McNamara all the while telling him it was a bad idea and he would be better off spending more time with his own children. He went ahead with the arrangement, encouraged by Allen.

It was an eventful few weeks. Knowing the principal, Cook arranged for Ryan to attend South Melbourne Tech. He would drop him off in the morning, collect him at lunchtime, give him a meal at the hotel, then return him to school.

According to Cook, Ryan got into an argument with a group of students, pulled out a .38 revolver and threatened to use it. The principal said Ryan had to go. McNamara has no memory of the incident. But she remembers that, a few days after being drummed out of the school, Ryan stole two Port Melbourne paperboys' bikes, selling them in Richmond. Cook asked him why he did it. 'Something to do,' he replied.

Cook had taken pity on the teenager — 'he grew up surrounded by drugs, guns and people being killed, so what hope did the poor little bugger have?' — and hoped to provide him with a more stable environment.

'I worded him up, you know — behave yourself, show a few manners, and chip in and help around the place,' he says. 'I was working on the theory there's no such thing as a bad boy. He was going all right — for about a week. In the end I couldn't do much more for him. He had to go back and live with Dennis Allen.'

McNamara says it was typical Cook, always trying to help others. But he couldn't help Ryan, who she remembers as a foul-mouthed and disrespectful teenager. At one point he demanded weekly pocket money of $300, saying that was what Allen gave him. He even tried to start a protection racket at the school in South Melbourne.

McNamara was relieved when he left. Soon she was leaving too, moving to a house in Albert Park. Another affair prompted it: she discovered Cook had slept with Allen's girlfriend. She told Allen, despite the danger it presented to her husband. 'I didn't give a shit. He'd hurt me once again and got with someone who was a smack addict. That was Fred. At the end of the day, I have no bitterness or regrets. That's life.'

When she left, Cook tried desperately to get her back, taking her to dinner for her birthday and giving her an expensive suede jacket. He even bugged her phone to see if she was talking to other men.

Pulling her car aside in a street in Port Melbourne, he saw a Carlton league footballer of Italian heritage with her and went into a rant: 'You ought to be fucking ashamed of yourself driving around with a wog in the car!' Cook found out McNamara had become attached to a helicopter pilot and said he would have Dennis Allen 'bury' him.

Kim McNamara says no-one could work out why her sister and Cook married. 'It was absolutely crazy. But you have absolutely no idea what Fred was like. He was very persuasive. He could sell ice to the Eskimos.'

Cook had already taken a fancy to another woman: 21-year-old Sally Desmond, a barmaid at the Chevron Hotel.

Sam Newman had asked Desmond out for dinner and took her to Cook's hotel. She supported Essendon, but her interest in football didn't extend to the VFA. She was unaware of Cook's deeds for Port

Melbourne — 'I had no idea who he was,' she says — but straight away took a shine to his charm, his looks, his generosity and a vulnerability that she thought he hid behind his ever-present humour. Soon she was keener on Cook than on his mate, Newman.

'I knew Sam was just after a fling,' she says. 'Put it this way: I didn't think he was the sort of bloke who wanted to get tied down in a hurry.'

Cook and Desmond saw each other for six weeks before he returned to McNamara and took the step of marriage. Desmond remembers that less than a month after the wedding, Cook visited her at her flat in Ormond.

They moved in together in January 1986, at a house in Yarraville — and she began to take drugs, too. 'That was my fault that she fell into a life of crime, definitely,' Cook says. 'I encouraged her. That's what you do when you're using drugs. You drag other people down to your standards.'

Desmond's brother, a police officer, was killed in a car accident in 1986. She was distraught when she returned to the flat after the funeral and accepted Cook's offer of speed. 'I weakened and said yes. It was one of the darkest days of my life, I guess,' she says.

Cook was taking a lot of drugs, but still thought he had his life under control. At Allen's house he watched heroin addicts come and go. Pretty girls would appear and two or three months later he would barely recognise them as they assumed the gaunt look of the addict, resorting to prostitution, bag snatching and other crimes to pay Allen for their drugs. He always asked them to bring him diamonds and gold, which he would have made into his own jewellery (Allen gifted Cook a thick gold chain with diamonds set around the letter 'F'. It was worth thousands of dollars, he said, so look after it. Months later, it was stolen from the Station Hotel).

'They'd become these pathetic, drug-dependent people,' Cook says of the young women. 'In hindsight, it was a terrible world. I couldn't see it back then. I was naïve. Bottom line, I had no idea what I was getting myself into.'

He remembers an addict and his girlfriend who were staying with Allen. He would give them a stolen car, a gun and the address of a building society. 'They'd go and bowl the joint over and come back with the money. He'd take out money for the heroin he was supplying to them and rent for living there, and they'd end up with next to nothing. And then he'd ring the coppers and put them in for doing the armed robbery,' Cook says.

Cook never imagined he'd sink to those depths. He was still reasonably fit and young, and believed he could stop using any day he wanted. He thought he could separate it from his everyday life, concealing it from family and friends.

But his business was suffering. He was spending less and less time at the Station. His brother Rodney had left in 1985. Fred Cook senior, who was a cleaner and odd-jobs man at the hotel, pleaded for his son to return, knowing his very presence kept the place ticking over.

Rumours about his drug use began to circulate around Port Melbourne. When challenged, he denied it.

A VFA official asked one of Cook's former teammates if there was anything he could do to help. Even then, Cook was the VFA's most valuable commodity. The official was told that if he tried to interfere he might well end up being thrown off Port Melbourne pier in concrete boots, so violent were Cook's associates. He was taken aback, but he had heard some 'heavy types' were frequenting the Station, scaring off the suits and sportsmen who had packed out the long lunches.

Cook had already lost his role at *World of Sport*, the television program that began in 1959 and evolved into a Melbourne institution. Mixing mainly football talk with barrel loads of banter, it was compulsory Sunday viewing. Former football champions Lou Richards, Jack Dyer and Bob Davis, racecaller Bill Collins, and prominent radio men Ron Casey and Doug Elliott were the pillars of the show. Segments included 'Club Corner', in which coaches would answer a few questions about the previous day's matches; the football panel, so often dominated by quip-filled exchanges between Dyer and Richards; the handball competition; and the woodchop, invariably won by a member of the O'Toole family.

The program engraved itself into the hearts and minds of Melburnians so deeply that even the sponsors of the guest giveaways, such as Patra orange juice, Tosca bags and luggage, and Ballantine's chocolates, became synonymous with the show. Richards called it one of the saddest days of his life when it wound up in March 1987, after 1355 episodes.

Reporter Stephen Phillips — who was the first pressman to talk to Cook after his heart attack a decade earlier, clinching the interview by taking in two cans of beer — got Cook the *World of Sport* gig and helped train him for TV.

He was 'a bit shaky' at the start, Phillips recalls, but quickly caught on. And he was comfortable in the presence of Richards, Dyer and Davis. 'He felt he had every right to be in that company,' Phillips says. 'At that stage he did. He was bigger than Hollywood.'

The first time Cook presented the VFA segment, someone mischievously put a hand near his groin, testing his composure before the cameras. Somehow, he made it through without saying 'balls' instead of 'footballs'.

'I had a fantastic time there,' Cook says. 'When the show was over we'd all have a drink and a laugh. Much the same as on the set.'

Cook blames a member of the *World of Sport* panel for him being dumped from the program. He says the panelist told a handful of other former footballers at a Channel 7 function that Cook was on heroin and that it got back to producer Gordon Bennett.

But that doesn't register with Bennett, who has been associated with Channel 7 all his working life. He says it was more a case of Cook failing to turn up as he 'self-disintegrated'. The station offered him help, but he said he would be okay.

'We never knew what was going on, but we knew it wasn't nice,' Bennett recalls. 'There was never any end, as such. Each week he came in and you'd talk to him and ask how it was all going. But we could see we couldn't put him to air any more, and he understood that. I don't think we ever pulled him aside and said, "Look, you can't do it." I think he just stopped coming in. The great Freddie … I get so upset about him because he had so much going for him.'

Bennett thought Cook did the VFA segment well, parading a 'big personality'. He had a face for television and his reputation as the star of the VFA gave credibility to his comments. 'We'd always had a VFA segment, and when Freddie Cook came on I was very happy to have him there because he sort of represented the whole VFA. We thought that was pretty bloody good,' Bennett says.

One *World of Sport* regular recalls Cook turning up on a Sunday morning talking 'Swahili'. 'He was mumbling something about a video. I couldn't understand a word he was saying,' he says. Phillips can't recall the specifics of Cook's exit from the program, but says it was 'probably messy'.

When Cook told Dennis Allen he had finished up at *World of Sport*, he was so enraged he threatened to 'knock' the panel member

Cook blamed for his departure. Cook says, 'I said, "No, no, no, Dennis, you can't do that, he's got kids." But he was serious. He wanted him gone, wanted to put a cap into him.'

Cook himself fired one of Allen's guns in a late-night incident at the Station Hotel. There had been a function upstairs and four car salesmen tried to leave with a beer box they'd filled with liqueurs. Cook fetched a .357 Magnum and confronted them outside, asking them to take the alcohol back in. 'What's that, a starting pistol?' one of the salesmen said with a laugh. Cook let go a shot into the asphalt a metre from him, but the bullet deflected into his shin. A pool of blood formed at his feet. The others quickly returned the box of liqueurs and, at Cook's urging, drove their mate to Prince Henry's Hospital.

People told him to steer clear of Allen. Early one morning police pulled over his car as he was leaving Allen's house. One of the officers told him, 'Fred, when are you going to wake up? Don't you know he's only using you for respectability?'

Cook didn't listen. He admits it was 'exciting, even exhilarating' to mix with Allen and his associates.

'It was a different world. I wasn't involved in the crime, but I was looking in on it. There'd be girls and prostitutes and drugs everywhere,' he says. 'It's like that line in the Peggy Lee song — is that all there is to a fire? There wasn't much I hadn't done on the right side of the law.'

From what Cook saw, no day at Stephenson Street passed without incident. One afternoon, Allen mistakenly took a hit of heroin instead of amphetamines and collapsed to the floor. Cook performed mouth-to-mouth and heart massage on him, until ambulance officers arrived and administered Narcan. Allen came to — and turned on the ambulance staff. Kath Pettingill gave Cook $1000 to keep them happy. He gave them something that pleased them more — his autograph —

and returned the money to Pettingill.

Around the same time, Cook heard something that still haunts him.

'Dennis Allen had a kid hanging around his joint. He was a bit slow. Allen got it in his head the kid was a police informer. He wasn't. He was just hanging around there giving Allen a chop-out, doing a few bits and pieces around the house. Anyway, we were sitting in the lounge room. Allen said I'd better go. That's what he always said to me when something was about to go down, "Fred, you better fuck off." By the time I'd gone out the front door, I heard *bang, bang, bang, bang, bang*, the tone of different gun shots.'

Cook bolted to his car. He heard no more about it. He didn't ask. He never saw the kid again.

Cook himself was twice on the end of Allen's violence.

He had been speaking to a South Melbourne police officer about a fundraiser for a sporting club. Word reached Allen that Cook was an informer. He sent three armed men to the Station Hotel to deal with him. They went up the stairs of the hotel and one crashed a portable video camera into Cook's face, opening a gash above his right eye. He was hopelessly outnumbered as they fought in the narrow hallway.

Summoning all his strength, Cook rammed two of the men into a wall, but they continued to land blows on him. Fortunately for him, Sam Newman had dropped in to the hotel. Told Cook was upstairs, he walked in on the assault and intervened. 'Sam stood between me and a gun and talked them out of it, defused the situation,' Cook says.

Newman regards it as the scariest day of his life. He says Cook had been horribly assaulted. 'They'd beaten the living shit out of him. They nearly killed him,' he says. 'He was fucked. I got a real shock. I'd never seen anything like that. It was surreal. You couldn't make a television show any more graphic.'

Newman fetched some towels and mopped up the blood from his mate's face. He said he would call an ambulance, but Cook said to leave it.

Newman rounded on the thugs after the attack, taunting them with the words, 'Well, aren't we big, strong, brave men?' One of them shot back: 'Don't get involved. Fuck off.'

As he walked out of the hotel after the confrontation, Newman was half expecting to be shot in the back of the head. 'But I wasn't going to leave without saying something. I remember thinking, *Yep, I'm not sure if I should do this, but if I don't I'll be selling my soul.*'

Later, when he was with Sally Desmond, Cook borrowed Kath Pettingill's car and brought it back a day earlier than was arranged. He entered the house and sat on the couch. Allen produced a pistol and whipped it across his face. Desmond jumped in.

'She saved my arse. She really did. She got up and stood between me and the gun,' Cook says. 'It was the right environment for Dennis Allen to shoot because there were a few of his friends there, all off their fucking heads, and he could have used them to clean up the mess. In normal circumstances, I wouldn't have let anyone smack me across the mouth. But that wasn't the time for me to fight back. He'd have put bullets into me, quick smart.'

Desmond was terrified as Allen went into a rage, which she says Pettingill set off by claiming Cook was going to steal the car. By that stage, Desmond says, he'd 'completely lost the plot, he was off the planet'. 'Dennis Allen thought everyone was against him, was crazy with paranoia because of all the shit he was taking. He threatened to blow both our heads off'.

Cook was surprised at how easily Allen got bail. But he learned he had two policemen in his pocket. Allen entrusted him with the job of paying them. Every Friday, one of the officers would drop in to the Station Hotel, have a steak and a salad washed down with a lemon squash, and wait for Cook to come downstairs with a fruiterer's brown paper bag fat with $3000.

By that stage, Allen and company were effectively using the hotel as a private clubhouse, storing drugs and guns in the safe and helping themselves to drinks. His former lawyer, Andrew Fraser, says Allen gave Cook money for a share of the business.

'Dennis was desperate to buy into it. He obsessed about it,' Fraser says. 'He paid Fred a whole lot of cash to buy in and the whole idea was for him to draw wages. Let's get one thing perfectly straight here: I wouldn't do any of that because it was illegal and I wouldn't do the documentation. I might have played it pretty hard in court, but I would never, ever, ever do anything that was dishonest.'

Cook can't recall how much money Allen gave him, nor what he did with it. He says he would have spent it on amphetamines, in keeping with his heavy use of it. 'No doubt I just pissed it up. Doesn't matter. It was Dennis Allen's money and he had plenty to go around.'

Desmond was shocked to be mixing with criminal company. She came from what she calls a 'protective background' and was as 'square as a butter box'. Her mother set her boundaries and expected them to be followed. They were: when she met Cook the only thing she'd done wrong was pick up a speeding ticket.

'To be introduced to blokes like Dennis Allen, seriously. They carried guns around and wouldn't hesitate to use them if you looked at them the wrong way,' she says. 'To go into that sort of world was pretty frightening. I met some pretty heavy sort of people.'

She occasionally thinks about the time Cook sent her to

Stephenson Street to buy amphetamines. When she arrived, Allen sent Jason Ryan out with a gun and keys, and told him to bring Desmond in and lock the gate behind him. He kept her there for nine hours. Cook went into a panic.

'I swear to God, Fred rang Dennis about 250 times that day, to see when I was coming home. He was worried he was going to do something. He had a bad rap for helping himself to women. He didn't kidnap me as such. He had me in the lounge room, but I wasn't going anywhere. He kept bullshitting to me, saying, "Well, I haven't got the keys, you'll have to wait for Ryan to come back," or "The stuff hasn't arrived yet so you can't go." It was a false imprisonment, but not a nasty false imprisonment, if that makes sense. I kept my cool. I was frightened, but I tried not show it. I went with the flow. Eventually, he gave me a whole gram of amphetamines and said see you later. After that, Fred never let me go over there on my own.'

On another occasion, a well-known criminal with a reputation for violence arrived at Allen's house to confront Cook over his treatment of Karen McNamara. Cook told him his marriage was his business. The criminal became irate, and as he paced back and forth across the lounge room Desmond noticed the butt of a gun in his overalls. She whispered as much to Cook and they quickly left.

Desmond was also caught up in an Allen rage involving Stevie Wright, frontman for the iconic rock band The Easybeats. Wright had fallen into a heroin addiction and was buying off Allen.

The way Cook tells it, Allen phoned the singer when he was in Melbourne for a gig and said he owed him $25,000. Wright apparently laughed him off with the words, 'Yeah, yeah, righto.'

Allen was so angry he rounded up some guns and ordered Desmond to drive him to the Tottenham Hotel in West Melbourne, where Wright was due to perform. Cook was in no doubt Allen would shoot Wright. He didn't want his girlfriend to be there when it happened.

He tried to reason with him. When that failed, he put his foot down and said Desmond wouldn't be driving the car.

'If it was going to be a murder, and the way Dennis Allen was talking there was every chance he was going to knock him [Wright], I didn't want Sally to be an accessory,' Cook says.

But Desmond credits Allen with giving her advice that served her well in the following few years: keep your mouth shut, be aware of what's happening around you, be careful who you trust. She suspects he took a shine to her because she wasn't a drug addict or a prostitute. 'I guess if he hadn't told me all that street-smart stuff, I wouldn't be here today,' she says.

When Cook opened the Station Hotel it was his pride and joy. But by late 1985, he says he was 'drug fucked' and concerned only about his next hit. He was beyond caring about the pub. His idea that he could turn his back on the drug when he wanted was a falsehood. He tried, but he felt sluggish. He needed it as a pick-me-up, 'to bring me back to life, make me feel better'. Amphetamines had initially been his way of getting through busy days. Now he couldn't go without it. In his own mind, he'd become an addict.

14

RUMOURS of Fred Cook's drug use became fact in December 1985. In a front page story headlined 'Footy Star's Drug Agony' in *The Sunday Press*, Scot Palmer revealed Cook was on speed.

Palmer started as a copy boy at *The Sun* in 1954. Newspaper ink ran through his veins. His father, Clyde, was one of Melbourne's top crime and sports writers, most notably at the *Truth*.

Clyde's brothers were also in the business of headlines and deadlines: Howard Palmer wrote *The Sun*'s popular 'A Place in the Sun' column for many years and Lindsay Palmer was sports editor of Sydney's *Daily Telegraph*. When he was on school holidays, Scot would serve as *Truth*'s copy boy, even becoming its first film critic, filing two or three paragraphs about the new big-screen attractions.

He developed a love for the VFA when covering it for *The Sun*, and made good contacts and lasting friendships at Port Melbourne. That was how he came to know Cook.

Palmer moved to *The Sunday Press* when it was established in the early 1970s, and quickly became its sports editor. He was probably the first newspaperman to make the move into television. Channel 7 would cross to him at half time during its Saturday night replay, and live from the Press office he would round up the news from the day's round of matches. His sign-off, 'keep punching', with his right fist clenched, became his signature move. And his 'Punchlines' column, carrying snappily written snippets from the world of football and photographs of pretty girls, was invariably the first place Press readers went.

Palmer covered nine Olympic Games, filing about the Munich Massacre and the Atlanta bombings. During his long career, he made scores of sources and broke dozens of major stories.

But it gave him no pleasure to reveal Cook's drug problem. He cannot recall how it came about — 'I'm not sure if he phoned me or I phoned him'. But he says it hit him 'like a bolt'. He was, and still is, fond of Fred Cook.

'Footy champion Fred Cook has been dozing eighteen hours a day as he completes withdrawal from a drug on which he has been dependent for a year,' Palmer wrote.

'Cook, the former goal kicking hero of Port Melbourne in the VFA, admitted to me he has been a constant user of the amphetamine known as "speed".

'He has lived through this year at "100 miles per hour" ... he became paranoid, aggressive and distrustful. Cook said the pressures of training and playing top-level VFA and operating his successful hotel in Port Melbourne had prompted him to use speed.'

Cook told Palmer he wanted to go public because 'so-called friends had been spreading stories about me being a heroin user and signing myself in to Odyssey House [a Victorian drug treatment centre]. I wouldn't even know the address of the place and I abhor everything connected with that vile drug. I've seen what it can do in the suburb where I live and I feel sorry for those people. An addict will sell their mother and then end up selling their soul to get the rotten stuff.'

He also told Palmer he had signed over the lease of the hotel (to a staff member and her husband). His proprietorship of the Station, so successful earlier, was over.

'Didn't really bother me at the time. That was my attitude. Didn't give a stuff about the pub,' Cook says.

In 1986, he went back and coached Footscray Tech Old Boys in the amateurs. He played the occasional good game, he says, but his drug problem was severe. It had reached the stage where he sometimes needed it to sleep.

'You'd take it and in the end your body would just give up. It was nothing to sleep for a couple of days on end. It [speed] was always in the back of your head. Always had to make sure the supply was there. Always had to be a step ahead. Didn't want to be caught unprepared.'

Cook never gave a moment's thought to being caught by police. He thought he was 'invincible'.

Events in September 1986 proved otherwise.

Cook and Desmond had moved into a house with a shopfront on Lygon Street, Brunswick, opposite the Red Robin socks factory. A contact at Channel 10 was giving him the master copies of tapes of old VFA matches, and he was running them off for supporters and selling them for $45 a pop. He was also selling drugs, as police soon learned.

He had put up $1500 bail for a man he knew as 'Chop Chop', who, with his girlfriend, began to live with Cook and Desmond at the house. Chop Chop borrowed Cook's car and was pulled over by police. They searched it, and found a screwdriver and pliers. In other words, he was 'equipped to steal'. Police also discovered a small amount of speed on him.

Asked where it came from, he said Fred Cook. 'He dropped me in the shit. But I would have got busted eventually,' Cook says.

Police weren't surprised at the information. Keeping Allen's properties under surveillance, they well knew he'd fallen in with a bad crowd.

It was just as well that police came calling. Weight had fallen off Cook and he was sick with Hepatitis C. When drug squad members raided the house on a Friday morning, he and Desmond were both in bed. Cook was barely able to move, the 'pathetic figure' he was later described as in court. He had been in bed for a week; Desmond had called a doctor to check on him.

The information supplied by Chop Chop was passed through the police chain of command. It resulted in an undercover officer being sent in to befriend Cook and buy drugs from him. The officer was Charlie Bezzina, who later wrote a book about his life as a crimefighter, as well as articles for *The Herald Sun* newspaper.

Cook insists he knew Bezzina was working undercover because Chop Chop had told him, saying, 'Watch out for him, I've seen him around somewhere. I think he might be a copper.'

But he was 'so far gone' he didn't care. In fact, he says, he didn't care if he lived or died. 'I was really low. Too many negatives, too many problems,' he says. 'I'd had enough. Yeah, I was lower than low.'

Bezzina wrote about the arrest in his book *The Job: Fighting Crime From The Frontline*, detailing how Cook had blown his cover.

Over two months, he wrote, he got to know Cook as a 'friendly, likeable guy; one of the rare nice guys in the drug world, if there's such a thing'. 'But he was a hopeless drug dealer; he couldn't do kilos, and his gear was very low quality because he was cutting it with so much other stuff. I actually felt sorry for him because he was down and out; a junkie who led a hand-to-needle existence.' He said Cook, who had been a 'fine specimen of athleticism and manhood', had 'deteriorated into a mere shell of his former self'. He was 'just a dickhead running with the wrong crowd'.

Cook confronted Bezzina with the words, 'Now listen, Charlie, I know you're a copper.' 'That's fuckin' bullshit,' Bezzina replied. 'Na, na, you're talkin' shit, mate.' Bezzina talked his way out of the house.

'But we decided it would be pointless to try to resurrect my business relationship with Fred because it was too far gone,' Bezzina wrote, adding that the case effectively ended his career as a covert detective because he could never be sure who Cook had told about him.

Bezzina says now that the man he regarded as 'the Teddy Whitten of Port Melbourne' and a 'likeable bloody rogue' wasn't out to be the next Tony Mokbel. He was making just enough money to buy speed and feed his and Sally's habit. 'The scourge of the drugs well and truly had him,' he says.

Bezzina speaks at corporate functions and uses Cook as an example of how drug addiction can bring down anyone. 'He went from the upper echelons of the community to being a nobody. So sad to see him come tumbling down like that. He was certainly in a bad space at that time.'

Cook and Sally were arrested and charged with trafficking, possessing and conspiring to traffic a drug of dependence. Television cameras were waiting outside the flat.

Sports journalist Jon Anderson wrote that, as he was led to the police van, Cook, 'forever the joker', held his hands in front of him as if waiting for handcuffs. He described Cook's body as 'wasted'.

Anderson, like many people, was unaware of Cook's drug addiction. But it explained his behaviour. One of the Station Hotel barmaids lived next door to Anderson. He sometimes saw Cook at her place and wondered why he always seemed to be on the move, jiggling his large bunch of keys or looking with suspicion over his shoulder,' Anderson wrote in *The Sunday Press* in 1988. 'As he later explained, they were some of the side effects of speed.'

Anderson had met Cook at the Station Hotel. 'He was really flying high in those days and he struck me as a likeable rogue who just had too much on his plate.'

Cook and Desmond appeared before the City Court on the day of their arrest. *The Sun* carried the news on page 5 in a story written by veteran police reporter Graeme 'Charlie' Walker, headlined 'Footy Star on Drug Counts'. Walker described Cook as 'thin and dishevelled and he had several days' growth of beard'.

Drug Squad detective Kevin Daffey told magistrate Brian Clothier that Cook and Desmond had sold five ounces of amphetamines in the past month.

Cook asked his father to put up $10,000 surety for his bail. He agreed. But he baulked at doing the same for Desmond. 'Fred, I don't even know the woman,' he said. Sam Newman came to her aid, and they were bailed on the condition they live at a house in Dromana and report to Mornington Police Station three times a week.

Cook remembers making a lot of calls trying to arrange bail for his girlfriend, but eventually he turned to Newman. He has since told the story that his old pal had female company when the phone rang, but Newman immediately put on his clothes and headed to the Melbourne Remand Centre, where he had some advice for Cook: 'Fred, why don't you apply to your life the discipline you applied to your football?'

The words have stayed with Cook like an old song. Newman would say them often over the years. He had no idea Cook had fallen so far into drugs. People had told him Cook was using them, but

Newman didn't recognise the signs, taking Cook's hyperactivity and 'up and about' demeanour as part of his personality.

'He lived pretty long hours. He put a lot of hours into the day and not a lot of sleep,' Newman says. 'But I saw no telltale signs, other than the fact his hotel had become a bit of a haven for the more anti-social elements in the community. I can only assume those elements of shadiness provided him with the substances.'

Newman remembers getting the phone call after Cook's arrest, stumping up $10,000 and speaking plainly with him. He says, 'It was along the lines of, "Fred, you wouldn't have got to where you did football-wise if you didn't have great discipline. It seems a complete paradox that you can be so undisciplined outside the football ground."'

But Newman suspected Cook knew what he was doing, and enjoyed it. 'It's hard to stop doing something you actually get a kick out of. The difference between a drug user and a drug addict is paramount. I think a drug addict is someone who can't get by without it. A drug user is someone who enjoys doing it occasionally or even quite a lot, but thinks they could stop if they had to. I think Fred fitted into that category. I think he thought he could stop if he had to. But he didn't want to.'

Bailed and broke, Cook and Desmond went to stay at her parents' flora and fauna park at Arthur's Seat on the Mornington Peninsula. They wanted to attempt a fresh start.

Cook was so tired and lethargic that he slept for six weeks. He was determined to get himself clean.

He was, for a time. But eventually he was drawn back to his old haunts, making trips to Melbourne to buy drugs.

In 1987, Cook returned to football, as coach of Crib Point in the Mornington Peninsula Nepean league. A Rosebud detective, Kelvin

'Tiny' Greenhill, had been contacted by Northcote colleagues to chase up Cook over bad cheques he passed a few months earlier when he was living in Brunswick. Greenhill went to Arthur's Seat to find a birthday in progress. Not wanting to embarrass Cook, he said he would wait in the car.

Cook emerged a short time later. They got talking about football. Greenhill had played at Crib Point and asked Cook if he would be interested in joining the club.

'So we worked out he'd have a kick,' Greenhill recalls. 'It added a bit of profile to the place. But he used to socialise pretty heavily. I think it cost them more to serve the grog up to him than it did to pay for him to play footy!'

Leo Cook, Crib's secretary at the time, confirms as much. Cook agreed to coach for nothing, 'but he had no money and probably cost me twice as much as any other coach at the time,' he says.

The appointment created a buzz around the town: more than eighty players attended the final training session before the first game and crowds increased dramatically.

Other clubs were also swept up in the excitement of the former VFA champion playing on the Peninsula. After matches, their players and supporters would seek him out in the social rooms, eager to buy him a drink and chat about football.

Crib had battled in 1986, but by the halfway mark of the 1987 season it had five wins and four losses, to be equal fourth on the ladder. Cook, telling his stories and jokes, had the Magpies eating out of his hand. 'With Fred around, it was like having a sportsman's night every Tuesday, Thursdays and Saturday. Gee, it was entertaining. No doubt about it, Sam Newman has obviously pinched a few of Fred's lines over the years,' Leo Cook says.

But the second half of the season was a disaster: the club lost nine consecutive matches. Its colourful coach had become unreliable, getting to training late or occasionally not at all. A handful of players responded by going elsewhere before the close of clearances.

Leo Cook has never forgotten an address Cook made at three-quarter time early in the run of losses. It was okay to lose, he said, as long as everyone had a 'red-hot go'. He said he wanted every player to be able to look him in the eye when they came off the ground at the end of the game. 'I'll be waiting at the gate,' he said. It was stirring stuff, like quite a few of his speeches.

When the siren went, the Crib Point players trudged off the ground. But Cook wasn't at the gate to ascertain who could look him in the eye — he was off socialising with opposition supporters. It didn't go down well with his players. Some said they wouldn't stick around if he coached the following year.

'He let himself down in the end,' Leo Cook says. 'Here he is with a side up and going, great numbers on the track, support everywhere and next thing you know … it was like looking after a kid in the end. I'd be getting phone calls like, "Don't tell Sally where I am." I think the temptation to duck up to town and burn the candle at both ends got the better of him.'

Desmond says he became bored once he regained his health. 'We were straight for a fair while. But Fred had time on his hands and started to creep back into it. And if he was using, I was using. I wasn't strong enough. I was crazy enough to believe him when he promised me we were going to give it away.'

Playing mainly in the ruck, Cook was handy in eighteen games for Crib Point, creating more goals than he kicked (fourteen).

But Crib people remember him more for his prodigious drinking than his football. He would take double shots of Bacardi, dirty it with a dash of Coke and bang it down. He could get through a large bottle and stay sober. 'He could friggin' drink, Fred,' Leo Cook says.

Before the end of the season, the club let Cook know it would be seeking another coach. But it took a while for the message to sink in: he would ring the secretary to talk about his plans for the 1988 season.

Leo Cook has thought a lot about Fred Cook's year at Crib Point, often with a chuckle. 'It's a season I'll never forget,' he says. 'It didn't work out in the end, but I don't think you could say it backfired. With who he was, he drew people to the club and brought in players.'

In the years since, the Cooks have bumped into each other a handful of times. 'And do you know, he's remembered my name straight away and talked to me like it was only yesterday,' Leo Cook says. 'I find that absolutely incredible.'

Greenhill had a soft spot for Cook, admiring what he had done at Port Melbourne and taking to his 'bigger-than-life personality'. But from time to time, he had to deal with him over what he calls 'a few misdemeanours'.

'The drugs were sort of like a disease to him. He just couldn't get off them,' Greenhill says. The policeman had known Bernie Balmer when Balmer was clerk of courts at Richmond and recommended Cook use him for legal advice. He had to use it often in the next few years as he struggled to stay drug-free.

In September 1987, he pleaded guilty in Prahran Magistrates' Court to two counts of assault. Women were the victims.

He had gone to the Chevron Hotel on a June night in 1986, and as he left at 3.50am he came across two friends of his estranged wife, Karen McNamara. One of the women abused Cook, who says he gave her an 'undignified clip across the back of the head'. He did the same to the other woman, who went to the aid of her friend. Cook was placed on a $1000 bond.

He was back in court the following month, after being charged with possessing amphetamines and conspiring to traffic in a drug of dependence. Police had raided a house he was frequenting at Hastings and found a small amount of speed. But their sniffer dogs failed to flush out the one-ounce packets of the drug he had put in socks on the clothesline. He also buried some amphetamines in the neighbour's backyard.

Overlooked for reappointment at Crib Point, Cook went to Dromana in 1988 and gave it good service. Mornington Peninsula football historian Doug Dyall has him down for fifty-six goals from eighteen games, putting him third on the league list.

In one match, Cook hardly touched the ball in the first half, prompting some theatre from Dromana coach Barry Evans. He marched on the ground after the half time siren and worded up his veteran forward about what would take place in the rooms. Evans would give Cook a fierce spray and threaten to start him on the bench in the third quarter. Cook had to demand to stay on the ground and promise to lift.

They staged it well. Cook even grabbed a towel and threw it on the floor of the changerooms after Evans had delivered his fake bake.

'You can imagine what the rooms were like,' Evans recalls with a laugh. 'All the other players got fired up, and the supporters joined in and the place erupted. Just an old coach's trick, that one.'

As he had at Crib Point, Cook increased home attendances sharply and made the most of his free drinks on Thursday and Saturday nights.

During the season he was interviewed by *The Sunday Press* man

Anderson, who had ghosted Cook's VFA column in the newspaper. The resultant article was titled 'How Footy Hero Fred Kicked The Habit'. But the headline was a long way from the truth. Cook continued to use speed on and off.

'I bullshitted a fair bit,' he says. 'I told people what they wanted to hear, that I was off the shit. I'd go a few weeks without it, then get back on it. People who knew I was using would come around and knock at the door. It was hard to keep away from it. Like I've always said, you could get drugs on the top of Ayers Rock if you wanted. But if anyone asked, especially the papers, I always said I was off.'

Sally had given birth to their first child, Jarryd, at Rosebud Hospital, and money was scarce as the family bounced around, renting houses at Dromana and Rosebud. Cook worked at Dromana Abattoirs for a few months, but was laid off, and registered for unemployment benefits.

The drug case was hanging over his head. The wheels of justice turned slowly, but it was finally heard in May 1989 before Judge John Hanlon. Cook and Desmond pleaded guilty to trafficking the amphetamines to undercover police officer Charlie Bezzina. Cook also pleaded guilty to four counts of having obtained financial advantage by deception, six counts of having obtained property by deception, one count of theft and one count of having handled stolen goods.

His counsel, Bruce Walmsley, told Judge Hanlon that Cook had been a 'very famous footballer in this state … and consequently enjoyed a high profile and no doubt enjoyed a pretty easy ride in life'.

'Each of them were in the grip of the drug as users. She [Desmond] was very much at the beck and call of the man she loved, and consequently ought to be qualified as less culpable.'

Desmond was given a three-year good behaviour bond. Cook received a twelve-month suspended sentence on the theft and deception charges, and a four-year bond on the drug charge.

Judge Hanlon told Cook: 'The punishment you have inflicted on yourself is greater than any punishment this court could serve upon you. If anybody looks at what happened to Frederick William Cook as a result of the abuse of drugs, they would never use drugs themselves.'

He warned him he would go to prison for twelve months if he breached the bond. Cook replied that the bond could be for twenty years and it wouldn't be broken.

He and Desmond had moved to Frankston and, always good with his hands, he picked up some maintenance work for Trotter Real Estate, owned by Bill Trotter. If a tenant reported a problem with the property, Cook would be called in to fix it.

Trotter was president of Frankston Bombers Football Club and urged Cook to have a run. He played eight games before an arm injury ended his season.

David Glennie, who was coaching the Bombers, says Cook did well despite being past the age of forty. 'Obviously, with his pedigree, we played him forward early on, but then we moved him into the ruck and his tap work was exceptional,' he says. 'His knowledge of the game and the way he read the game made up for a lack of athletic prowess. He was a solid contributor.'

Glennie remembers a match in which, before the bounce of the ball, Cook had declared to teammate David 'Bluey' Geddes that he would hit a running Glennie on the chest with a tap, and the Bombers would stream forward and kick a goal. That was precisely how it played out. As Glennie ran downfield, all he could hear was Cook yelling, 'See Bluey, I told you that would happen!'

Off the field, Cook enlivened the Bombers' social scene with his fund of football yarns. He drew people to him and could have them laughing all night.

'Imagine this: if you walked into any football club or cricket club across the state right now and there were fifty people in the room, you'd probably find a large circle with ten blokes listening to one bloke. And that bloke would be Fred,' Glennie says. 'He was very charismatic, had an amazing set of stories — he could tell them for two days if he wanted to — and he was good company. I'm glad I met him. I enjoyed his contribution.'

Glennie himself can tell a great story about Cook. The real estate firm asked him to attend a property with a faulty heater. The tenant was a football supporter and immediately identified Cook as the great Port Melbourne full forward. They steadily drank their way through two bottles of top-shelf liquor. Cook left after midnight — without having fixed the heater.

But not a year after he told Judge Hanlon he could impose a twenty-year bond and he wouldn't break it, he did — and all because, he says, he was trying to help an elderly woman keep dogs out of her vegetable patch.

He was sent to the woman's place to repair a flywire door and leaking tap. She soon complained that dogs from next door were making a mess of the vegetables she was growing in her backyard.

'She was crying. She was upset. Those veggies were her pride and joy,' Cook says. He offered to build an attractive fence with double gates to keep them out.

He went to a Frankston hardware store, put red gum posts, pine timber and a bag of cement in the back of his car and drove off without paying. The way he tells it, he worked for two-and-a-bit days on the fence. The woman was most appreciative — and paid him with a cup of tea and a Butternut Snap biscuit.

The hardware store had reported the drive-off to police. They charged Cook with theft and he was fined $600 in Frankston Magistrates' Court. But the case meant he had breached the bond given to him almost twelve months earlier. He had also been charged with tampering with Telecom equipment, rigging up a phone from a neighbouring property. A date was set for him to appear at the Victorian County Court: 27 April 1990.

Before then, Cook did a two-part question-and-answer series with Sam Newman in *The Sun*. Reading a revealing piece with the singer Cher in *Playboy* magazine, Newman got the idea of pulling off similar interviews with sporting subjects, first selecting Hawthorn player Dermott Brereton.

He took the transcript to the editor of *The Sun*, Colin Duck, who was impressed at the uncompromising questions and blunt answers, and decided to run it. Other interviews followed. They gained a big following and were given splash treatment in the news section. It was the first dollar Newman had earned since striking financial trouble when he backed a friend at the bank. When the business failed, the bank called up Newman's guarantee. 'I was absolutely penniless,' he says.

For eighteen months he lived in a room at the back of the Ascot Vale home of his best friend, Kevin King. 'He put me up until I was able to claw my way back,' Newman says. 'I wasn't bankrupt, I didn't owe money to anyone, but I didn't have any myself.' *The Sun* interviews helped establish Newman as the media performer he is today.

He gradually broadened his range, going from footballers like Brereton, Tony Lockett and Peter Daicos, to other sportsmen and sportswomen, politicians and entertainers. He asked a grumpy Eartha Kitt what he would need to do to take her on a date. Noting the cap on Newman's head, she replied: 'You can take that fucking cap off for a start!' Then she leant back, laughed and said she had never been asked that question. The interview went well.

Shaping up to Cook, Newman gave his old mate no favours, tossing questions at him like grenades. They covered football, drugs and sex.

Newman opened part one with: 'You said you'd rather die than quit. Quit what, exactly?'

Cook replied with: 'Playing football.'

Newman: 'I see. I thought it may have been the drugs you were on.'

Cook: 'I had a heart attack in 1972 and I think the doctors are always very pessimistic in their diagnosis at times like that. But I was young and immature, and I felt all right — well, football was my life.'

Newman: 'You've certainly given your heart the ultimate loyalty test since then. I can't recall anyone who's had such a contrasting life.'

Newman kicked off part two with: 'Talk about drugs in sport — you've really played everyone on a break.'

Cook: 'Someone gave me some speed one day when I had a cold and it cleared my nose. Let's just clarify one thing. I played twenty-odd years of football without drugs and I never used them to enhance my football performance.'

Newman: 'Never?'

Cook: 'Never ever. I've been on anti-inflammatory drugs, like anyone else, but contrary to a lot of rumours the only drug I ever took was speed — amphetamines.'

Newman: 'Didn't you use heroin?'

Cook: 'Never taken heroin in my life. It abhors me.'

Newman: 'So why did you start taking speed?'

Cook: 'It was a combination of things. My lifestyle was such that in any given week I was running a hotel, playing football and training five nights a week, writing for *The Sunday Press*, working on 3DB, doing *World of Sport* on Sundays, plus appearing at two or three sportsman's nights a week. In the end I needed about six more hours a day than there was. Without drugs, in this world there'd be a lot of sick people — there are some benefits. Drugs are okay, providing you use them and they don't use you. In the end, I became dependent on them mentally because they kept me awake and alert. The downside is you don't eat, you become paranoid and your health suffers, so consequently you can't make rational decisions.'

Newman: 'You seem to be justifying the fact you turned to drugs.'

Cook: 'I'm giving you the reason why. By the same token, the drug I got hooked on was originally prescribed as a weight control, but became infamous because of truck drivers abusing it — to stay awake for long periods.'

The interview came to women, with Newman asking: 'Was it important for your image as a high-rolling playboy to have two to three girls a day?'

Cook: 'What do you mean?'

Newman: 'You had a fair entourage for a while.'

Cook: 'It was an occupational hazard, I suppose, being in the type of business I was. There was tremendous opportunity for a girl to make a huge amount of money for taking her clothes off — with no physical contact.'

Newman: 'Did you personally interview all the applicants?'

Cook: 'Most of them. Okay, all of them, but you're only as good as your staff, so I had a vested interest in picking the right people.'

Newman: 'I put it to you, you've made a disgrace of your life.'

Cook: 'Do you want the short answer? Yes.'

But Newman has always stayed close to Cook. He points out they were from 'very different walks of life' — Newman attended Geelong Grammar and Cook went to Footscray Tech — but they always got along. Video footage exists of Newman's fortieth birthday party, at which they drink and peel off one-liners in the company of a bevy of blondes.

'Fred's probably like me, takes people as you meet them. I found him good and fun company, a loveable larrikin, a thoroughly pleasant man,' Newman says. 'I have this very simple philosophy. It probably gets me in trouble occasionally. But being friends with someone is unconditional. You're friends with them no matter what they do. Unless, of course, they do horrendous things. A lot of people are fair-weather friends, don't like to be associated with others when controversy or infamy hits them. I'm not one of those people, probably because I expect my friends to treat me that way as well. So I've stuck by him. I know his foibles, his idiosyncrasies, I know his failings. But, let's be honest. Everyone has those. Your friends are your friends, your acquaintances are those who like to come in and out of your life. Fred Cook is a friend.'

Lawyer Bernie Balmer says Newman has been one of the few constants in Cook's life in the past thirty years. 'Shit, hasn't Sam been through the wringer trying to keep tabs with this fella?' he says. 'I mean, he hasn't exactly lived a quiet life, our Fred.'

15

HE had heard the roars of the crowd and felt the slap of thousands of hands on his back.

Fred Cook relished playing football and feeling that 'buzz in the belly'. He enjoyed just as much the adulation that accompanied his prodigious goalkicking for Port Melbourne.

But what happened after the shouting had died away, after his deeds were done and his race was run? Cook says there was an emptiness in his life. The euphoria had gone, apparently forever. When he retired from the VFA, he was still a significant public figure. Sally Desmond saw as much when she walked down the street with him. Women would approach and say, 'Fred, I used to watch you on TV and I was in love with you.' Men would tell him what a great footballer he had been, how they had seen him take those marks and kick all those goals. Desmond was staggered at the reverence he received.

But it was nothing like the cheers at VFA grounds. They were a sweet harmony to his ears. He would take a mark and a split second later spectators were on their feet applauding, clapping hard again when he kicked a goal. His actions caused thousands of reactions. A mere clap of his hands and a wave of his arms towards the boundary was enough to send spectators scrambling back to their vantage points after they had dashed onto the ground to celebrate his one hundredth goal.

It was a 'weird and wonderful feeling', he says. Where else could he gain a comparable experience? Cook says that when he retired he replaced the sensation of playing with taking drugs. Later, the same fate befell a string of high-profile AFL players. Others sought solace from alcohol. Others still slipped into depression when removed from the pedestal upon which even average footballers are placed.

Recognising the problem, the AFL Players Association runs a range of programs to help players make the transition back to everyday citizens once their careers have ended. The issue is hardly exclusive to football. Sportsmen and sportswomen the world over have felt the sense of loss.

The US writer and former college footballer John Ed Bradley wrote about it beautifully in his book *It Never Rains in Tiger Stadium*, describing the pull of the game. He left football at age twenty and feared that 'nothing I did for the rest of my life would equal those days when I played for LSU … what if I never had it better than when I ran out under the goalposts on a Saturday night, the crowd on its feet, my teammates all around?'

After the VFA, Cook says 'stimulation' was missing from his life. 'Happened overnight, really. It was there one day, gone the next, thanks for coming. Football was my whole life. Once it was gone, I was lost. I had to find that big buzz somewhere else.'

Professor Jayashri Kulkarni, the director of the Monash Alfred Psychiatry Research Centre, says many sportspeople are without the coping mechanisms when they recede from the spotlight and no longer have a 'special position in the community'.

For some, it's a process akin to grieving the death of a family member or friend. They miss the thrill of competition and lose financial security, a sense of entitlement and public recognition.

'They might love–hate it, but they get used to it and then it goes,' Professor Kulkarni says. 'So there has to be a grieving, and like any situation of grief some people use drugs or alcohol to cope. That's not helpful and it leads to a host of other problems. Each individual is going to have their responses, depending on their background and their own support systems or lack of support systems.'

Umpire Frank Vergona often wondered what would become of Cook when he finished playing. Vergona got to know him well and saw that he 'loved and thrived on the limelight and adulation. It was always going to be a worry when it wasn't there anymore,' he says. 'I only thought about it because I knew how much he enjoyed being a big name. But I never expected him to go into such a dark hole.'

Cook missed the routine and structure of football: training three nights a week, playing on weekends, attending club functions and promotions. It required discipline to stick to the schedule, keep himself in good shape and stay at the top of the goalkicking charts. When it was no longer there, he 'sort of bumbled along'.

'I ticked all the boxes to go down the wrong path,' Cook says. 'I had time on my hands, I had money and I had a bit of fame. Bad combination for someone looking for a bit of excitement.'

He yearned to get back to the club and enjoy the blokey banter with teammates, and the togetherness that goes with team sport, individuals coming together in pursuit of a collective goal. That was where he was most comfortable, holding court at Port.

Who tried to pull him back from the path he had taken, using drugs and consorting with criminals? A few people, he says. But it didn't matter, because he didn't want to listen. As he sat high on that pedestal he rarely heard the word 'no'. Fred Cook did as he pleased.

In an *Age* article in 2014, North Melbourne champion Wayne Carey used similar words to Cook — 'buzz', 'emptiness', 'routine' — as he reflected on his travails after his football career.

Carey wrote that he never thought he would struggle after retirement. He did — 'big time'. There was a 'massive hole' in his life. 'In some ways it was like losing family. Which is exactly how I viewed the players and staff at Arden Street — as one big family. But one day, sometimes without warning, it all gets taken from you, just like that,' Carey wrote. 'And you're left with this feeling of emptiness … and then reality sets in … what the hell am I going to do with the rest of my life?'

Sally Desmond believes the final siren on Cook's career led him towards drugs, more than the need to find a few more hours in the day to get through his commitments.

'I don't care what anyone says. The drugs replaced his football career,' she says. 'Definitely. They filled a hole in his heart. They gave him the high that he couldn't get from the footy — and he has an addictive personality.'

Kim McNamara, Cook's former sister-in-law, agrees. She says Cook was a 'broken man' when Port Melbourne moved him on. She believes the Borough administration should have handled the departure better. 'It hurt, it hurt, it hurt,' she says. 'That's why I've always felt an understanding with him. I knew where his problems were coming from.'

Phil Cleary led a more rounded life than Cook, but he too experienced a void when he stopped playing for Coburg. Coaching the Burgers filled some of it, but it couldn't produce the adrenaline charge of snapping a goal or using his pace, dipping his shoulder and hitting a pack like a missile.

The 'sheer exhilaration of that contest out there on a big paddock' cannot be ignored, he says. 'When I was no longer playing, it was difficult for me. But I coached and I had premierships. Then I had another sort of premiership, when I won a seat in Federal Parliament. But when I left Parliament I was disappointed and found it hard to replace the adrenaline rushes I'd had, firstly with football and then politics. And there I was without it any more. Even I was thinking, *Gee, I need excitement in my life*.' For a time, he was a 'cork in the ocean'.

As Cook says, football was his life and brought him a multitude of openings. When it ended, a fog set over him. He had the hotel. But he always thought there would be more for him than standing behind a bar pouring drinks and telling stories. He imagined building a portfolio of properties and living in luxury on the Gold Coast. But it slipped away with his drug problem. His earning opportunities dried up once his addiction became public. The phone that once never stopped ringing stayed silent.

Desmond says that for a long time Cook was unwilling to knuckle down to the daily routine of dragging himself out of bed and going to work. She saw a man looking for a 'free pass' because he had been a champion footballer.

'I'm sure that was his attitude to a lot of things in life. He'd paid his taxes — $300,000 in one year — so he thought everything should come to him free,' she says. 'He seemed to think work was beneath him. For him to go and work, that wasn't going to happen, not unless someone was going to pay him thousands of dollars a week to do it. All he had was football and the stuff that came with it. When that was gone he didn't have a trade or a profession to fall back on. He couldn't melt back into society.'

As the years passed, so did the warm glow of fame. He is still recognised — people over the age of, say, forty will point him out as he sits in Mornington Park reading the newspaper and drawing on a cigarette — but the heyday and pay day of 'Fred Cook, Superstar' have long gone.

Desmond says she cannot comprehend what it would be like to have a large profile and watch time slowly diminish it. 'He was already retired when I met him. He still went to the Good Friday Appeal — I went to it twice with him, I think — and he was pretty big there. But gradually that sort of stopped.'

Pam Cook has thought over and over about her brother's slide. She believes he handled the fame football brought him, but found it difficult 'coming down from being important'.

'How can I put this? He always wanted to work at a higher level, I suppose. He didn't want to be doing the day-to-day stuff that everybody else does. So if he could get out of it he would ... like his job at Puma, he had freedom as the promotions manager to go and do what he liked. And when that stopped, and when the football stopped, he found it very difficult.'

ı|Iı

IN the Victorian County Court on 27 April 1990, Fred Cook's fall from champion footballer, popular publican and media performer had its landing in a jail term. Judge John Hanlon revoked the suspended sentence and told Cook: 'My faith in you is shaken.'

Herald court reporter Derek Ballantine wrote that Cook 'bowed his head and choked back tears'.

His counsel, John Clohesy, said Cook intended to pay for the hardware goods when he had money. Referring to his parlous financial state, he added: 'There was no milk in the house and his wife was crying because there were no nappies for the baby.'

Local MP Burwyn Davidson and senior Frankston ambulance officer Terry Grange provided character evidence. Grange told how Cook had helped raise $40,000 for a fund for children with brain injuries.

Sun reporter Russell Robinson sought comment on Cook's plight from his old friend Ted Whitten. 'Maybe this [jail] could help him,' Whitten said of the man he always called 'Bucket', short for 'bucket mouth'. 'I was his first coach when he played at Footscray and I was saddened for the boy that this happened. I'm sure he'll be a different person and will have learned his lesson.'

Desmond had remembered the judge's warning that Cook would go to prison for twelve months if he breached the bond. She replayed the words over and over, and on the way to court told Cook he might not be coming home.

'Nah, nah, I'll be fine. I'll be right,' he replied, apparently not comprehending the gravity of the situation. 'He was thinking that because he'd got off last time he'd get off this time,' Desmond says.

She was expecting the worst, but the jail term hit her like a sledgehammer. They had been inseparable ever since taking the flat at Yarraville. She couldn't recall them being apart for even one night.

'It was a real kick in the butt for me,' she says. 'I had a two-year-old son to look after by myself. Fred was shocked. I think it suddenly hit him that his whole freedom had gone.'

Desmond now believes a longer sentence — two or three years — would have been better for Cook, giving him more time to reflect on the consequences of his drug use. She is adamant he didn't do the 'hard time' needed to deter him from reoffending.

After the court case, Desmond found work at a service station in Frankston, putting Jarryd in child care while she did 9am to 9pm shifts five days a week. On Sundays she would drive to Morwell River Prison Farm, where Cook was transferred from the Melbourne Remand Centre.

'I battled on as best I could,' Desmond says. 'I couldn't just curl up and die in a corner because Fred had gone to jail. I had a child. I had to get on with it. That was life with Fred Cook. I loved him and that was that.'

ı|lı

BEHIND the headlines of Fred Cook's drug addiction and imprisonment was a family devastated at how his life had unravelled so swiftly.

Cook's parents and siblings took enormous pride in his VFL and VFA careers. Shirley Cook usually stayed at home and listened to games on the radio, although she had attended a night grand final her son played in for Footscray, happily doing her knitting. But she would prepare a big Sunday lunch for her husband and children before sending them off to Port Melbourne matches.

The girls, Lynette and Pam, became ardent Borough barrackers. Pam maintained a scrapbook, and a few of the pages found a place in Fred Cook's old blue suitcase.

'We were all very proud of him, proud that he was at the top of his game. We enjoyed being a part of it,' Pam says. 'We gained a great deal of pleasure watching him play and seeing the success he was bringing not only to himself, but to all the fans at Port Melbourne. It was pretty tough there for a while. I had the Bulldogs on Saturday and Port on Sunday. I had two footy matches to go to and I was trying to do HSC [Year 12].'

Fred Cook senior rarely missed a match, and 'doted' on his son, according to former Port Melbourne ruckman Brendan Behan. You wouldn't see a prouder father, he says.

The family was distraught when it became apparent Cook had a drug addiction. Pam likens his slide to a train losing its brakes. 'It was going so fast and it was uncontrollable, and if you got in the way you ended up going with him or otherwise you had to leave him alone,' she says.

'I remember at the time ... I had young kids and I didn't want to be associating with him because of the people I knew he was associating with. I thought, *Well, you can handle that, but the rest of us have to get out of the way.* We tried to help, always tried to maintain contact, mostly by role-modelling or suggesting better outcomes. But he was just like a snowball rolling downhill and getting bigger and bigger, and there was no way out for him. Only he could do it. He needed good people in his life and he chose not to go with good people. He chose to keep some fairly horrific company, which made it worse.

'There was nothing we could do as a family but hope he would turn his life around. It was disappointing for my mum and dad. They shook their heads many a time and said, "What can we do?" But there was nothing they could do. He was an adult who'd made his own path.'

In hindsight, she says, she should have known of her brother's problems earlier. She had seen the erratic behaviour, the fast speech, 'the go-go-go kind of attitude and lifestyle'. She adds: 'I'm surprised he's still alive. I thought he'd be dead at forty.'

Pam remembers her brother's generosity. When she was a girl he took her to the Royal Melbourne Show and said he would buy her as many bags as she could carry. She went home with them hanging off her arms.

After he had married Bernadette, Cook still popped around to the family home in Yarraville. Pam looked forward to his visits. She held her twenty-first birthday at Fred and Bernadette's home in Avondale Heights, guests mingling by the pool. Cook lost his licence for speeding when he was working at Puma, and Pam drove him around for three months after she graduated from Teachers College.

She kept a distance from Cook when he was in the grip of his drug addiction, but 'I was always there, because he's my brother'. It caused friction with other family members, but she was mindful of not taking sides. Pam visited him in jail, taking her children to see 'Uncle Fred'. 'It was always a daunting experience. I'd say, "You never want to be in there." But I was showing them loyalty and the fact that you stick by people when hard times come.'

Cook was largely oblivious to the hurt he was causing his family. He was 'caught up in my own little world'. 'Your family slips down your list of priorities when you're a junkie,' he says. 'Sad, but true. You can't see the consequences of what you're doing.'

Years later, he's still feeling the consequences. Of the children from his first marriage, he has little to do with Jacqueline, is on good terms with Tracie, but has no contact with Nathan, who he last saw on his sixteenth birthday when he dropped around with a $50 note. Cook has six grandchildren but rarely sees them. He has never set eyes on Nathan's three children.

He speaks regularly with Rodney and Pam, but less often with Lynette, who was angered and disappointed at his behaviour. They were estranged for a long time.

When Fred Cook senior died in 2008 at age eighty-four, Rodney said at the funeral that young Fred had taken the family to its greatest high, but also its deepest low. The words resonated with his sisters. It crushed them to see him go from champion footballer to prisoner.

Shirley Cook died in August 1988, but her eldest son has little memory of the funeral — he admits he went there high on speed and hadn't slept for a week. Pam says, 'He has told me that. But by that stage it was just normal for us to see him like that.'

ı|lı

FRED Cook was confident he'd be going home with Sally Desmond and their son Jarryd after the court case. Instead, Frederick William Cook, forty-two, was taken to Pentridge Prison, still in the suit he wore before Judge Hanlon.

In three years, he had lost most of the things he enjoyed as a high-profile footballer. Now he'd lost his liberty, restrained by the bluestone walls of the historic Melbourne jail.

Cook spent one night at Pentridge. He arrived after lock-down and was taken to a dark cell where an inmate was watching television. He rose from his bed and offered Cook a 'bong'. Ten minutes later, the new prisoner was high on marijuana. 'I could have been at a Jesuit church or a boy scout hall. It was hash. Fuck me down dead, I didn't know where I was,' Cook says.

The following day he was transferred to Melbourne Remand Centre, which had opened the previous year and mainly accommodated offenders awaiting trial or classification within the prison system. Where a few years earlier he mixed with entertainment and sporting figures, now he kept company with armed robbers and even murderers.

At the remand centre, some of the other men in custody recognised Cook as the champion Port Melbourne footballer and sought to make his acquaintance. He was forever being offered cigarettes, especially by notorious criminal Richard Mladenich (who was shot dead at St Kilda's Esquire Motel in 2000). Mladenich would assault other prisoners and give their smokes to Cook, who would quietly return them later. 'I was embarrassed at how much he tried to please me,' he says.

But Cook caught a bigger break than free cigarettes — the governor of the centre, Colin Marston, was a keen football follower and gave him kitchen duties, a privileged position. Cook repaid the favour by organising a sportsman's night in the gymnasium. Ted Whitten, Bob Skilton and Cook himself were the speakers.

He had his own cell, which had a toilet, shower and television. He would get up at 7am, take breakfast, then start cooking meals. A session in the gym and visiting time followed. Lock-up was at 8pm. It was a relatively cosy arrangement compared to what he knew of Pentridge. Desmond thought it was 'like a holiday'.

In his first few weeks at the remand centre, Whitten and his old Port Melbourne teammate David 'Sam' Holt were among Cook's handful of visitors. According to Skilton, Whitten was saddened at Cook's decline. 'He was disappointed in the fact that Freddie didn't do what he said he was going to: clean himself up,' he says. 'We were all good friends and we wanted to do what we could for Freddie, but at the end of the day it was up to him. He was too talented to be wasting a life like that.'

Holt remembers that Cook hardly stopped talking during the one-hour visit, not wanting the conversation to turn to his sentence.

'Fred didn't mention it and neither did I,' he says. 'It wasn't good to have to go and see him in those circumstances, but unfortunately that's where he was. It didn't get much better for a fair while.'

Holt was like a lot of people — he believed Cook could have given up drugs if he tried hard enough. He pined for the 'old Fred', the knockabout bloke always rattling off stories and drawing laughs.

But Holt came to see it wasn't as easy as saying 'enough'. Cook was in the grip of an addiction. 'Some of the things he did, that wasn't Fred. That was the drugs coming out of him,' he says. 'I knew what the real Fred was like. He was always a great bloke. The drugs changed him, unfortunately. I always hoped he'd work his way through it.'

Other former teammates were less sympathetic. Holt has heard ex-Port Melbourne players overlook Cook when discussing the club's great players. He says it can only be because of his drug-taking. 'A few people who were close to him were anti-drugs,' he says. 'So in their minds Fred had done a very bad thing and they soured towards him. But I could understand his predicament.'

Cook knew he'd let many friends down, 'immensely'. 'I didn't really think about it before I went inside, because I was off my head,' he says. 'But I'd let a lot of them [friendships] dwindle away. People were obviously disappointed in me. I see it now. I'd more or less brought humiliation, and I suppose sadness, to the people around me.'

One was his son Robert, then fourteen, who was teased at school about his father going to jail. Cook wrote a letter to him, and Robert visited him the next day.

Fred Cook senior had told his son a spell in prison would be good for him, as he would be isolated from drugs.

In fact, the remand centre was awash with them, as *The Age* reported in October 1989. It quoted Marston as saying that prisoners were putting pressure on relatives to smuggle drugs into the centre.

At the time, prison officers were unable to search visitors without their permission.

Cook remembers a young offender swallowing bags of heroin, and putting others up his back passage. Prisoners, itching for a hit, sweated on him passing them, trying to speed up the process by pouring soapy water down his throat.

'There was more of it, and of a better quality, than anywhere out on the streets,' he says. 'It was everywhere. That was the environment. It hardly encouraged someone to try rehabilitation.'

In June, Cook was taken back to court to face the telephone charges. He pleaded guilty in Melbourne Magistrates' Court to rigging up his disconnected phone to his neighbour's line. Jarryd, choking, vomiting and having difficulty breathing, had been taken to Rosebud Hospital. Cook told Telecom investigators his phone had been cut off and he was desperate to stay in touch with his son. He was fined $500 for making $20 worth of calls in twelve days.

Later that month, Cook was transferred to Morwell Prison Farm, where the first instruction he received was to serve as captain and coach of the football team in a match against Won Wron Prison (Morwell won by four goals).

He was put on an outdoor gang, planting trees in winter and slashing grass in summer. During one clearing, he and other prisoners stumbled across a flourishing marijuana crop. Tempted to start stripping its leaves and smoking them, they nonetheless told their guards and were given the job of loading it into vans.

The former Station Hotel proprietor was also Morwell River's unofficial publican, selling cans of smuggled-in beer for $2.

Despite being in prison, Cook got another headline in *The Sun* when Morwell East Football Club made noises about recruiting him for a few games in the Mid-Gippsland league.

'We've heard that there could be financial reasons stopping him playing,' club secretary John Hehir told the newspaper. 'Because he has to turn up to matches with a prison officer there could be penalty payments. But Morwell East is prepared to meet the costs.'

The plan fell through. But soon Cook was tangled up in talk about another sporting challenge: a boxing match with fellow former footballer Mark 'Jacko' Jackson.

At the remand centre, Cook did some boxing under veteran trainer Brian Levier, who as an old Port Melbourne supporter took an interest in him and was impressed with his skills. Levier had also trained Jackson, and he came up with the idea of putting them in the ring in a heavyweight bout.

'I rang one of the papers and said I'd like to see it happen, and next thing you know it's all over the news and every bastard is ringing me!' Levier, seventy-one, chortles. 'I hadn't even told Fred about it. He read it in the paper. He said to me, "I don't want to fight Jacko! He's mad."'

Levier says Cook was a strong man who hit hard and would have been a decent boxer if he had pursued it at a younger age.

The fight never eventuated. But for Cook, freedom did. On Monday 17 December 1990, he walked out of Morwell River, declaring the jail sentence to be his first and last.

'If you get addicted to drugs it's not a problem — it's a catastrophe,' he told reporters dispatched to Gippsland to interview him.

He said he was planning to marry Sally Desmond, that he was looking forward to spending time with Jarryd, would like to resume playing football and had received three firm sport-related job offers.

Cook was optimistic about his future. Lifting weights, he got himself supremely fit at Melbourne Remand Centre and Morwell, and wanted to stay that way. He thought things were looking up. But drugs were soon to pull him down again.

When he was in jail, Desmond continued to work full-time and had moved to a unit in Addicott Street, Frankston, owned by her boss at the service station.

After his release, Cook did a few odd jobs, but mostly stayed at home with Jarryd. Desmond became pregnant with their second child.

She says it wasn't long before he was flirting with speed again. 'Someone introduced him back to the shit [drugs] and he was off,' she says. 'That was his problem. He wasn't working a lot. He was too busy being bored. You get bored and start hanging around with the wrong crowd. One thing leads to another.'

In April 1991, she returned from work after an afternoon shift at the service station. She'd been home thirty minutes when the family dog, a German Shepherd named Sam, began acting up at the front door.

Desmond told Cook he should take a look at what the dog was barking at, but he said there was nothing outside. There was: police from the Frankston District Support Group. They knocked at the door. Cook told them there was nothing in the house that would interest them, but eventually he went to a drawer in his bedroom and pulled out a small amount of amphetamines, as well as some marijuana he'd been selling. Jarryd vomited on his blanket, upset at the sight of police preparing to take his father away.

Cook was charged with possession, use and trafficking of cannabis, and possession of amphetamines.

He was bailed, but a fortnight later he was again before Judge

Hanlon for breaching the earlier bond. Adjourning the hearing until the other charges were resolved, the judge told Cook: 'The reason your appearances before me are acquiring as many episodes as a television soap opera is entirely to be found in your behaviour.'

His behaviour deteriorated. The way Desmond tells it, his use of speed became heavier and he began selling it in large quantities. 'He was going downhill fast,' she says.

Cook had also rented the unit next door to store stolen property brought to him in exchange for drugs. There were chainsaws, lawn mowers, video recorders, computers, televisions and other household appliances. Cook, or a speed addict he used as a 'runner', would sell the items to a bayside pawn shop that asked no questions.

When the Portsea holiday home of a Melbourne television personality and comedian was burgled, the items finished up in Cook's hands, washing machine and all. Two teenagers hooked on amphetamines virtually emptied the place.

Around that time, Cook made a trip to Mordialloc to buy speed and cannabis, taking Jarryd and the dog with him. When he went inside he told a teenager at the house to keep an eye on Jarryd in the backyard. The drug deal done, he went outside a few minutes later to collect his son. But he had disappeared. The property had no fence to separate it from the railway line. Traffic on the Nepean Highway was busy. Cook panicked, sprinting up streets in search of the boy.

Despite having just bought drugs, he rang the police. Three cars arrived. 'He wouldn't go anywhere without the German Shepherd,' Cook told them. 'You mean this one?' a female officer said, pointing to Sam. The dog led the search party to a large hole dug in readiness for a septic tank. Jarryd was at the bottom of it. 'Sam pushed me in,' the frightened youngster said.

That night, when she returned from work, Cook told Desmond what had happened. She was of a mind to strangle him, angry he had allowed their son to wander from the property.

'Incomprehensible, really. I was absolutely furious. But I had no control over him at that stage,' she says. 'He was on his own axis. He was out of control. I was pregnant, still working and trying to get my head together for the sake of the kids. It was full-on.'

She thought the death of his mother three years earlier contributed to Cook's spiralling state. He regularly expressed anguish about it, saying it was unfair that, as a non-smoker, she was taken by lung cancer when still relatively young. A few weeks before she died, Shirley Cook had held baby Jarryd in her arms and told her son, 'Please, look after him, Fred.'

'His whole world collapsed,' Desmond says. 'He took it really bad. Crushed him. We had a pretty bad habit, then we got it together. When his mum died, that was the beginning of the end in my eyes. He fell apart. He wouldn't go and see her that much before she died. He wanted to remember her how she was. I guess he was embarrassed at what he'd become. I think he could have come back from Brunswick [the arrest] if he hadn't lost his mum. I really do. His mum was his world, a good, strong woman and his backbone.'

Cook's way of coping, she says, was to put a needle in his arm and hope the pain would go away. 'But it didn't matter how much shit he put in, it was still there.'

On 10 December 1991, Cook again felt the cold slap of handcuffs around his wrists.

Police from the Frankston District Support Group had been watching the comings and goings from Addicott Street for three months and moved in. They seized amphetamines and $10,000 worth of stolen goods. There was also a running sheet detailing which items had been brought in and paid for with speed.

Cook was charged with four counts of trafficking drugs, possessing and use of drugs, and possession of stolen goods. He appeared before Frankston Magistrates' Court, where the police prosecutor, Senior Constable Mick Barry, opposed bail, pointing out Cook was already on bail for the earlier drug charges and also had the suspended sentence hanging over his head.

Cook was remanded and taken to Pentridge Prison. Two weeks after his arrest, Desmond, Jarryd and newborn Jordan were evicted from the Addicott Street unit. She had no money, but a neighbour took her and the children in until she could move in with her sister in Coburg.

At the time of his arrest, Cook was owed $9500 by buyers. 'He kept giving everyone "tick", free drugs. They all knew he was a big softie. There was no way known they were going to pay him,' Desmond says.

Approaching Christmas, Pentridge was in lock-down, owing to a prison officers' strike. Cook was kept in his cell for all but one hour of the day. Distressed at the prospect of another jail term and having fought with Desmond, he thought about taking his own life.

'I'm sitting there thinking, *Fuck it all.* Sally wasn't talking to me. I thought she'd gone and would piss off with the kids. I was utterly depressed. I'd had enough,' he says. 'But it's no big deal to think about suicide. It's when you start sitting down to plan it all out that you've got problems. But I'm too much of a coward to do it.'

Cook received his second jail sentence on 22 January 1992. He pleaded guilty to twelve charges, including trafficking, possessing and using a drug of dependence, and handling stolen goods.

His counsel, Charles Nikakis, asked magistrate Lionel Winton-

Smith to give Cook 'one last chance'. But Winton-Smith, calling the man before him a 'tragic and broken' figure at 'the crossroads', jailed him for eighteen months and fined him $1050.

He was taken to Pentridge, going from the yards to B division and A division.

If Cook found comforts in his first sentence at the Melbourne Remand Centre and Morwell Prison Farm, there were none to be had at Pentridge, especially in the yards. He put his hands out the trap door at 6.45am, was let out for breakfast between 7.30am and 8.30am, had a light lunch at 11.30am, mustered for a hot meal at 3pm and was locked down from 3.30pm. On warm days the heat from the bluestone bricks was unrelenting. Cook worked for $28 a week, sweeping cells, transporting meals and, in A Division, growing vegetables.

He found a friendly and familiar face in B Division: his old Preston opponent, the fearless and feared Harold Martin.

Martin was an education officer at Pentridge and well knew the harsh environment Cook had entered. He pulled him aside and told him he needed to be careful about the company he kept and to go about prison life quietly.

'Coming from the outside where he was protected and a hero, he could have been at risk among some pretty heavy sort of blokes,' Martin says. 'He just had to play it low-key and not get involved in any criminal activity within the confines of the jail.'

Martin had always been fond of Cook, remembering a gift of Puma football boots and a trip to Tasmania for a 1980 representative match (when Cook, apparently in recognition of him being the star of the touring party, was placed in superior accommodation to his teammates).

He was sad to see a 'true legend of the VFA' doing time. 'But it didn't make him any worse of a person because he'd come across bad times. I just tried to advise him and give him support. He was in a heavy part of the jail. A lot of action went on in there.'

Martin thought Cook's standing as a former football star would make him popular with prisoners. But he worried he would also be seen as a 'scalp' among inmates seeking to make their name in Pentridge, 'mugs who wanted to whack Fred Cook'. Martin himself had encountered such a situation when, walking out of the Preston ground with his wife, he was assailed by an opposition supporter carrying a gun.

Cook did strike trouble, spending three days in the prison hospital after being assaulted. An acquaintance asked him to deal with an inmate who was flaunting a nude photo of his daughter. In return, he was offered a quantity of drugs. Cook wasn't interested but passed it on to another prisoner, who duly carried out the assault. But when there was a delay in handing over the drugs, the prisoner arranged a beating for Cook. Three men set upon him in his cell, covering him in bruises and cutting his face.

In 1993, Phil Cleary signed the visitors' book at Pentridge. The lives of the VFA stars had taken divergent paths. The bluestone-wall setting of their meeting was near the Coburg City Oval, where years earlier Cleary had watched in awe as Cook put his teammate Ron Beattie on the rack. Now, the Coburg No. 18 was an independent Federal member of Parliament, having won the seat of Wills in 1992, succeeding former Prime Minister Bob Hawke. Few doubted his exploits at Coburg had contributed to his victory. Pentridge Prison was in his electorate and his celebrated former opponent was its best-known occupant.

They didn't talk politics; they nattered happily about the old days, with Cleary reminding Cook of some of the Coburg–Port Melbourne clashes that had occurred down the road.

'I'm of left politics. I believe in compassion and rehabilitation. Fred was a petty crim, nothing worse. He was down on his luck and he deserved a compassionate ear,' he says.

Cook appreciated the visit. But he has one regret: he never got around to asking his local MP if he could try to have his sentence reduced by a few months. 'The little bugger had gone by the time I remembered to ask,' he says.

Cook played in a prison match on the A Division oval and by half time had kicked sixteen goals. When the siren went, his humbled opponent looked at him hard and said, 'If you kick one more goal on me I'll shiv [stab] ya.' Cook asked to sit out the rest of the game, saying he had twisted his ankle.

ı||ı

GETTING by on a sole parent allowance, Desmond had moved to West Coburg to live with relatives and be closer to her partner. She remained loyal to Cook, despite their rows and her family's misgivings. She was prepared to stick it out, believing he had finally reached his rock bottom.

People often asked her why Cook couldn't stay off drugs, believing it was as easy as him saying no. She knew differently; she had experienced the daily enticement to use, gaining strength from resistance, but often giving into temptation.

'It's an illness, a disease. You fight with it constantly,' she says. 'I'm clean now, but it took me a long while to get there. You can slip back into it. You might slip back into it once or twice. Okay, that's a hiccup. But if you're not strong enough to say, "Hey, what are you doing, do you really want to keep going down this path?" you're back on it. You're always vulnerable. If you've got nothing to look forward to, no love coming, no people who care about you and you're just going in the same direction, what's the use of getting off it if you really enjoy having it? There's something missing in their life, or something happened to them, and they start taking it as a recreational thing and all of a sudden it becomes a full-time thing.'

Cook and Desmond called themselves 'co-dependents'. 'I'd say no, he'd say yes. And then he'd say no and I'd say, "Aww, come on, don't be like that, it's all right for you when you want it." And, bang, next thing you know you're going to get on. And before you know it you're back in that familiar territory, you're back on that path. And that's how you live until someone says you're under arrest or there's no more money left, until something's put in your way to make you stop.'

For Cook, that was prison. Desmond thought they could rebuild their lives when he was released, perhaps get married and fly to a tropical island for their honeymoon.

The distance between them became greater when he was transferred to Loddon Prison near Castlemaine. It necessitated more long drives for Desmond and the children, but she never failed to go.

Cook was made a maintenance man at Loddon. But he was still being sought for media interviews. A reporter and film crew from a current affairs program visited him. Cook made it memorable by saying he'd never seen so many crack amateur lawyers. With film rolling he yelled, 'Righto, you guys, how many of you are innocent?' Every arm around him shot into the air. The footage was used to promote the interview.

While Cook was at Loddon, Desmond also received a jail sentence, over the December 1991 raid at Addicott Street. She was charged with possession of amphetamines. Found guilty, she was sent to jail for nine days for breaching an earlier bond. 'You have seen what has become of Cook through misuse of these drugs,' Judge Hanlon told her.

ı|||ı

ON his release from Loddon, Cook joined Desmond and the children at a house at Fawkner. She had saved enough money for a bond and to clear their bills. She hoped they could finally settle into domestic harmony.

'Like every other jail promise he made, he said he was going to keep off the gear. But he didn't. The same old thing happened not long after he got out. He was back on the gear, and off and running again,' Desmond says.

The next few years were chaotic, as he continued to take drugs and they lurched from house to house. Cook initially picked up some work at a building site at Ascot Vale, but used what money he made to buy amphetamines.

The couple's relationship had also become violent. As far back as their time living at Yarraville, Cook had given his partner what he calls a 'bit of a clip' and 'a bit of a backhander across the back of the head'.

Desmond says there were slaps and forceful pushes, but more than once he went at her with a clenched fist. 'It was usually when he had the speed in him or was coming down,' she says. 'Fred's not a violent man. You could not find a kinder, nicer bloke. He'd give you the shirt on his back in a blizzard. But the drugs brought out an ugly side of him. Not that he ever really punched me. If he had, he would have killed me.'

She would forgive him, placated by his assurances it wouldn't happen again.

Evicted from Fawkner when they were unable to pay the rent, Cook, Desmond and the boys were forced to go to a shelter for the homeless in South Melbourne, their only possessions the clothes they were wearing and whatever they were able to fit in the boot of their car. The real estate agent took their furniture, bedding and even some of Cook's football memorabilia. 'We lost everything, basically,' Desmond says. 'It was devastating.'

After four weeks they moved to a house in Altona, arranged by welfare agency Hanover.

16

WITH a drug addiction and two stints in prison behind him, the days of Fred Cook being called a 'hero' had long passed. The description 'disgraced former footballer' had replaced it.

But the hero tag settled over him again when he helped save a man from a burning car in Altona in March 1994. It put him on the front page of a late edition of *The Herald Sun*.

Two young men had stolen a Holden Commodore and used it in a smash-and-grab at a Spotswood newsagency. Police saw the car soon after and gave chase, dropping off when the Commodore touched speeds of 150 kilometres per hour.

The car hit a gutter, rolled and smashed into a tree at Altona North. Cook was sleeping when he heard the bang. He threw on a pair of jeans and ran to the scene, about fifty metres away.

Its engine revving, the Commodore was upside down, with one of the men inside. Cook crawled in through a smashed window, giving no thought to the possibility of the.vehicle exploding.

'You don't think about it at the time. If you did I suppose you'd have second thoughts,' he told *The Herald Sun*. 'I did think while I was in the car that I hoped if the situation was reversed he'd do the same for me.'

A fireman who arrived told him the car could burst into flames, but he stayed in it, yanking at the ignition wiring until he cut off the engine. He then worked with a rookie policeman to free the man, who was pinned between the crushed roof and seats, and had suffered horrific facial injuries.

Cook himself was bloodied when he crawled out, counting the cuts and scratches as he sat on the roadside. The adrenaline rush of the rescue was one thing. He'd also taken speed that night. The dual effect of his body's hormones and the artificial stimulants left him panting for breath.

When he regained it, he remembered the $4 in coins he'd put in his pocket for milk and bread in the morning. They'd fallen out while he was in the car. Money stolen from the newsagency was scattered on the road, so he picked up $4. A police sergeant late arriving to the crash saw him and said it was despicable to loot a crime scene. Cook flared up, explaining he was replacing only what he'd lost. Another police officer intervened, telling the sergeant about Cook's role in getting the injured man out of the car. Apologies were made.

Cook was even told he'd be put up for a bravery award. He said it was unwarranted. Still, it was the first time in a few years that he'd been on good terms with the police. It wasn't to last.

A few days after the incident, Cook and Desmond rowed. It got physical and she called the police, who urged her to charge him with assault and take out an intervention order. She did, and the police came back to arrest Cook. He returned that night, climbing through a window and begging Desmond to let him stay. She called the police. Cook had hidden on the garage roof, but was eventually found.

'He'd lost the plot,' she says. 'He was hanging around with a known drug dealer and the drugs were free flowing. If Fred did stuff for this dealer, ran errands or whatever, he'd get thrown a quarter [ounce] or a half. When drugs are that available, you take them. Fred was an addict. He took them. He wouldn't make the commitment to give it up. I'd try to get him to make a commitment when he wasn't on it. He'd always make a commitment when he was on it. But he loved it too much for it to ever happen.'

Desmond fled with the children to a refuge centre. But the couple reconciled. She went to court at Williamstown and had the intervention order struck out.

Desmond remained 'madly in love' with Cook, and nothing was going to keep her away from him. They spent a few weeks at a Williamstown caravan park, then went to different addresses in Ascot Vale, Cook dossing with his drug associate.

Then came something more permanent, a Ministry of Housing property at Hastings that Desmond furnished with belongings she had in storage.

Cook also returned to an old haunt: Port Melbourne Football Club. In June of 1995, he was back at the North Port Oval for the first time since he'd been asked to retire, to line up in a legends match. Until then, he'd been too embarrassed to attend the club he had served so spectacularly. He found it uncomfortable to talk about his descent into drugs, and worried there would be questions or even admonishments about it.

'I thought it was best to stay away and keep out of everyone's way,' he says. 'In hindsight, some people around there might have been a help. But I didn't want to ask for help. I was too big for that.'

Before the game Cook said the crowd would be expecting nothing less than ten goals from him. He said he'd hopefully kick them by half time, then slip into the bar.

He got 'four or five'. He also got a lot of pleasure from slipping on the Borough jumper and running out again with players like Sam Holt and Billy Swan. He was half expecting Old Man Goss to deliver a blunt appraisal of his performance as he came off the ground.

ı|lı

ANOTHER raid, another arrest, more charges, back to court, the threat of another jail term.

Fred Cook was still unable to resist the drug that had caused him enormous pain and damage. The act of putting white powder on a spoon, adding water, heating it with a cigarette lighter until it was soluble, drawing the substance into a needle and releasing it into his arm was irresistible.

A feeling of euphoria washed over him almost immediately. The cares of his world would disappear. There was nothing like it. He's often described it as 'instant gratification'. The scars on the crease of his elbows show he found it often. 'I'd hate to think how many times I did it,' Cook says. 'It was just like having a beer.'

Inevitably, police caught up with him again. He was charged with possessing amphetamines. And he was charged again soon after with trafficking, possessing and using both amphetamines and cannabis, as well as handling stolen goods.

Cook answered the single charge at Broadmeadows Magistrates' Court in September of 1995, receiving a suspended sentence. He was also directed to present to a drug and alcohol treatment centre as an in-patient.

Lawyer Bernier Balmer had pushed for the treatment, telling magistrate Peter Mealy that Cook needed rehabilitation and he would personally drive him to Windana if the court saw fit to release him.

He attended the Windana centre at St Kilda, only to leave after four weeks. It put him in breach of the court order. But he presented daily to a Peninsula drug counsellor, who arranged for him to return to Windana, this time at its large property at Pakenham.

Eating fruit and vegetables, joining in discussion groups, helping prepare the weekly budget, submitting to urine tests and working on general maintenance, Cook stayed clean.

The other charges were dealt with at Melbourne Magistrates' Court in October. He was again given a suspended jail sentence and ordered to remain at Windana.

The Herald Sun reported that 'things might have finally turned around for the former VFA football champion Fred Cook, who narrowly escaped going to jail on drug trafficking charges'. Cook told the newspaper he could 'really see a light at the end of the tunnel'. He said, 'In the past, it was just, I'll see what happens. I'm really positive about my life now.'

Referring to Windana, he said, 'You can't do it on your own. I was too proud to ask for help in the past. Far too proud. You know, I was a footballer, I've won football matches on my own, I don't need any support to get off drugs. But I was wrong, I was wrong.'

Desmond was expecting the couple's third child when he completed his stint at Windana in November 1995. At age forty-eight, Cook was thinking not only about fatherhood, but making a return to football.

He did, lining up for Tyabb for a few games early in 1996. He kicked two goals in his first match for the Yabbies, who were coached by former Melbourne backman Jamie Duursma.

Growing up, Duursma spent many Sunday afternoons in front of the television, watching Cook put on a show in Port Melbourne games. He could hardly believe it when, encouraged by the wife of a club official he'd encountered in the Tyabb post office, the man he admired as 'Fabulous Fred' turned up before the season and said he'd like to have a run.

Duursma says Cook was 'fantastic' with the club's many young players, demonstrating forward play and ruck work. He also encouraged them to lead a healthy lifestyle, holding himself up as an example of how drugs could ruin people. He confided he'd put more than $2 million worth of amphetamines into his body.

'He was great with the kids, Freddie,' Duursma says. 'He'd pull them aside and tell them not to make the mistakes he'd made. He told them how he'd stuffed up, how he'd had a massive fall from grace, and didn't want to see any of them go down that same path. They never did. They all went on the straight and narrow. You can put a bit of that down to what Freddie told them.'

Desmond took in the Tyabb games with newborn daughter Jaimee, and Jarryd and Jordan, along with Neroli Campbell, a troubled teenager who had started living with the couple (they came to regard her as their own daughter and were devastated when she died in a car accident in 2010, leaving behind five children).

Jarryd watched with pride as his father chased a kick. Cook, believing there were no greater bores in life than old footballers who rattled off stories about their younger-day exploits, spoke infrequently about his career to his children and displayed no memorabilia in the family home. But, hearing snatches of stories from people and coming across newspaper articles, Jarryd began to appreciate his father's stature in the game.

One of his school friends said his dad played for Hastings. 'Well, my dad is a legend,' Jarryd shot back. He started playing in the juniors at Tyabb.

Jarryd showed his old man's marking ability. But Cook says he lacked the pace to go to higher reaches of the game. 'Too slow over the first ten yards, the boy. But geez, he could take a catch. Only needed one grab at it. Bang. Straight in the mitts.' He was as proud as a peacock when Jarryd finished second in league and club best and fairests.

Occasionally, the youngster's name attracted heckling from the fence. In one game, he took a fine mark. A spectator yelled, 'Are you on drugs, Cook? No wonder you're playing well. Any chance I can buy some off your old man?' Jarryd slowly walked over to him and said: 'I wouldn't sell anything to you. You've got a big mouth.' The retort silenced the spruiker.

His father had rarely joined him in kick-to-kick sessions in the street. It took a lot of cajoling from Desmond to get Cook out of the house. 'Mum was probably a better kick than dad,' Jarryd says. 'She had six brothers and knew what she was doing. Maybe dad was too embarrassed because of what had happened.'

Called on by local schools, Cook had started to lecture students about the dangers of drugs. He stood before them and said he was living proof how they destroyed lives, relating his decline from champion footballer, hotelier and sportsman's night fixture, to addict and prisoner. It was a tale of excess more often associated with musicians and movie stars. But Cook had also started taking speed again. He admits there were times when he injected with amphetamines in schoolyards before going into classrooms for his talk.

'I knew what I was talking about and everything I said was damn well true. But I couldn't practise what I preached,' he says.

The family was forced to move from Hastings to Safety Beach in 1997 after Desmond's friendship with another woman soured and she was assaulted, twice suffering injuries to her teeth. There was also a string of threats, prompting Desmond to take out a restraining order against the woman.

The Safety Beach property had a backyard shed, and Cook used it to grow marijuana plants. Affected by speed, he would often get up in the middle of the night, throw the shed doors open and tend to the plants. 'He'd light up the backyard like ET was landing and think no-one was watching him,' Desmond says. He harvested two crops, making about $14,000 from each, and had a third going when police arrived at the house one morning.

Cook was charged with cultivating and possessing cannabis. This time his legal man Bernie Balmer couldn't convince the court to impose a suspended sentence. Pleading guilty in the Dromana Magistrates' Court, he copped a three-month jail term, his third for drug offences.

Cook was sent to Beechworth, telling Jarryd, Jordan and Jaimee that he was going to Queensland to work for a while.

Once more he worked outdoors on maintenance, building a rockery at the prison entrance. Another time he was sent to clear an elderly woman's backyard after the death of her husband. He had been a keen home brewer, setting the alcohol content of his drop at six percent. Cook and his gang came across dozens of stubbies in the backyard and steadily drank them all.

The bulk of the stories Cook tells about his time in jail are coated with humour and involve him skirting the rules. But no day passed without him wishing he could walk out the gates and merge back into the world from which he'd been removed.

'It sort of crushes you, not being able to do your own thing,' he says. 'You do what the guards and the prison system tell you to do. Everyone does. A bit like a flock of sheep, really. I couldn't have done a big lag [sentence]. When it's six months or nine months there's always that little bit of light at the end of the tunnel. If it was two or three years I'm not sure how I would have got through it.'

This time Desmond didn't maintain the long-distance dedication. She wanted to provide more for the three children and had tired of Cook's drug-taking, the court appearances and constant financial struggles. There had already been two brief separations and intervention orders, but she was thinking of leaving him.

'It was getting to the point where I'd just had enough,' she says. 'I mean, how long can you keep going like that? Our lives had been a mess for a long time. I was sick of it.'

Yet in March 1999, not long after Cook was released from Beechworth, the couple married at the Melbourne Registry Office.

Desmond's sister Wendy had given her the engagement and wedding rings from her first marriage, and was a bridesmaid, as was Neroli. Desmond made sure her parents were there, figuring it would be the only time she married.

Afterwards, the couple had a quick drink at a Brunswick hotel before spending the night at Ascot Vale. They returned to Safety Beach the next day. There was no honeymoon. Desmond also says there was no proposal from Cook. A friend had suggested they get married. 'Well, what do you reckon?' he asked.

'I'd always wanted to get married. Every girl does,' she says. 'So of course I said yes. Fred had been married twice and been divorced, so it was no big deal for him. I wanted him to get married earlier. I had an engagement ring and a dress when he was in Morwell, and he was going to marry me when he got out. But he never went through with it. Drugs always seemed to get in the way of everything that should have been normal in the relationship.'

There was another move, to Essendon, when Cook accepted a position with a business trying to branch into flip-over mobile signs. It was the first time he'd had regular employment for fifteen years and he was earning 'good eating money'. When the venture failed he tried a start-up signage operation with a car wholesaler in North Melbourne, taking his former sister-in-law, Kim McNamara, with him.

After a few months at Essendon, Desmond returned to Safety Beach with the children, but without her husband. 'I couldn't deal with it any more, the violence, the drugs. I just wanted out,' she says. 'I was done with him.'

Cook stayed in Melbourne, living with McNamara at her home in Port Melbourne. She had known him since she was nineteen and they had maintained friendly relations despite his stormy marriage to Karen. 'He had the arse out of his pants. He was putting his head down here, there and everywhere. I felt a bit sorry for him, really,' she says.

Cook would have the children on weekends and they would sleep over. But McNamara says he was a 'nightmare' to live with. He would go to bed at 6pm, get up at 2am, go out and leave the house open. She would berate him and he would leave, but he'd soon be back. He had nowhere else to go.

Always a sweet-tooth, he was arrested in South Melbourne after opening a bag of Freddo Frogs in a supermarket, eating a few and giving others to passing children. Taken to St Kilda Police Station on a busy Friday night, he was sent home with a warning to pay for his chocolates next time.

After a break of about eighteen months, Cook and Desmond made their peace and he joined her back at Safety Beach.

Neroli, Desmond says, had encouraged her to reunite with

her husband. She came from a broken home and wanted to see the couple try to resolve their differences for the sake of the children. Neroli always had a soft spot for the man she called 'Pa'. They shared an open and honest relationship. She often told him he had to get his act together.

ılı

ASIDE from the legends match, Cook for a long time had little to do with the competition he bestrode in the 1970s and 1980s. But on a whim he phoned the VFA's successor, the VFL, and asked to attend the 2001 count of the J. J. Liston Trophy, the award he'd won twenty-one years earlier at Yarraville. He took Sally Desmond and his son Robert Rapkin.

The league had undergone a revamp in 2000, taking in AFL reserves teams, and had been operating as the VFL for five years, to the displeasure of VFA loyalists.

Cook spoke to VFL general manager Martin Stillman about his invitation. 'Mate, what have you done to my competition?' he asked. 'I left it in good hands. We had crowds of 20,000 and you've fucked it up around me.'

The league had been asking Cook along every year, but, changing address so often, he never received the Liston invitations.

Cook was fidgety when he walked into the function at Rod Laver Arena. Arriving early, he collected his name badge, took a lemon squash from a waiter and shuffled to the right of the entrance. One hand cradled his drink and the other was buried in the pocket of his suit. He was apprehensive.

Gradually the foyer began to fill, and gradually people saw Cook and walked over for a chat. He was soon at ease. At one point, he placed his drink on the carpet and put his hands in the air as if preparing to take a mark, the badly bent fingers held high. He was spinning his stories again.

Later in the day his presence at the count was announced by the MC: 'And ladies and gentleman, it's great to see the former Port Melbourne champion Fabulous Fred Cook here.' Sustained applause followed.

Interviewed by *Leader Newspapers* a fortnight later, Cook said how much he had enjoyed the occasion and a moment back in the limelight.

He also spoke about his drug addiction, using the past tense. 'I choose not to use because I don't like the consequences,' he said. 'If you could prove to me here and now that I could enjoy amphetamines and have a normal, happy co-existence with my family and friends, I would use it today.'

Cook said the prospect of not having a relationship with his wife and children had prompted him to get clean. He told a story about daughter Jaimee falling asleep on the couch. Cook picked her up to put her in bed. She flopped her arms around him, opened her eyes, said 'Daddy, I love you,' and fell back to sleep. 'The feeling, the tingle I got in my stomach, I couldn't get that in a syringe. That's the difference.'

But the truth was that Cook was continuing to use, on and off.

Two months after his Liston appearance, Jarryd, then thirteen, was injured when he fell twelve metres down a cliff as he played at Dromana beach with ten-year-old Jordan. Landing on rocks, he suffered a shattered collarbone, a bruised lung and head injuries. Jordan scrambled to the beach below, dragged his brother out of the water and ran back to the road for help. Jarryd was taken to the

Royal Children's Hospital. Jordan later received a bravery award for his actions.

'Yesterday, I didn't believe in God, but now I'm not so sure,' Cook told *The Herald Sun*. The newspaper published a photograph of him and Desmond looking suitably relieved as they held Jarryd's hand in hospital. But many eyes were drawn to Cook's smile. It revealed that his once-immaculate teeth were badly decaying, a legacy of his years of drug use.

Cook had been named in Port Melbourne's team of the century in 2003. At a premiership celebration two years later, he received a medallion acknowledging his six flags.

Offstage, he told the host of the function, his old pal Stephen Phillips, that he wanted to auction the medallion and donate the money back to the club. Phillips said it would be inappropriate, telling Cook he would cut off the interview if there was any mention of an auction.

'As he started talking, I actually put my hand underneath his coat and took hold of his belt,' Phillips says. 'I was going to drag him straight off the microphone and say, "Ladies and gentlemen, put your hands together ..."'

Like many people, Phillips was saddened by the decline of a man he thought had so much going for him. 'What happened to Fred was a tragedy,' he says. 'There's no other word for it.'

17

SALLY Desmond left Fred Cook for good in late 2004, saying she was going to live with her parents. But she'd quietly arranged to relocate to Horsham, almost 400 kilometres away, taking Jordan and Jaimee with her. She wanted to take Jarryd, but his friends were on the Mornington Peninsula, so he went to live with her brother. Three months later, he joined Cook in a caravan park at Dromana.

Desmond didn't really want to go, believing the separation could be stressful for the children. She was loathe to take them away from Cook. She saw he loved them deeply, would do anything to protect them and would miss the daily contact with them. And she still loved her husband. 'I would have died for the man. I would have taken a bullet for him, I would have gone to jail for life for him,' she says. 'That's the God truth. I would have done anything for him. But I had to let go.'

More than twenty years after Dennis Allen had tipped amphetamines into his drink at the Station Hotel, Cook was still using it.

'Enough was enough. It was time for me to get my shit together and grow up,' Desmond says. 'I had to go. It was sink or swim. I had children I had to grow old for. I sat them down and told them. Fred was still tampering with drugs. He needed perspective in his life, some reality. He was never going to get that when I was still around to look after him.'

Desmond had turned forty and had four children. But she thought she had nothing else to show for her life. For too long she'd been living like a mouse in the shadow of Fred Cook. 'I was always being a "yes" person. There was no respect for a lot of the years. He's so much older than me, and more manipulative. He's a great manipulator. He gets what he wants, when he wants it. I was young and stupid and naïve and innocent in a lot of ways. He took advantage of that. He's says it was love, but I don't know about that.'

For almost a year Cook had no idea where his wife had gone. 'Where are ya?' he would growl when she phoned. He repeatedly accused her of 'stealing my kids'. Desmond put them on the train on school holidays so they could spend time with their father.

'I wasn't happy when she went,' Cook says. 'But she'd had enough. Fair enough. We'd been fighting a lot and I suppose I always thought I was right. The situation with the kids was the thing that got to me. When you're involved with them twenty-four hours a day, doing the little things, like making sure they've had a bath or been tucked into bed or done their homework, it hurts like hell when they've gone. But I had to get on with it. When Sally pissed off, the sky didn't fall in.'

Cook and Desmond have remained close since their separation. She says they're 'great mates' and speak on the phone most days. When she calls, the name 'Supa' flashes up on his mobile. They haven't divorced and Cook often refers to her as 'my wife'. There is a light that has never gone out; he admits he still loves her.

They have a relationship that works better when they're apart, Jarryd says. 'They laugh and they joke, but they can't live in each other's pockets. It gets to a boiling point, sometimes even these days. Mum can put up with it because she knows she can put the phone down, go back to her life and unwind.'

Desmond says she couldn't live under the same roof as Cook again. If she did she would end up killing him. She says he likes to be 'baby sat' and is too set in old-school ways. 'He comes from that era where the woman looks after the man. He expects to be waited on and he's totally bloody irresponsible.'

With his wife and children gone, Cook went to the caravan park in Dromana. Jarryd joined him a few months later, and father and son battled through as best they could. Cook, in and out of work, would often steal food to get by.

He had been doing it for a few years, placing supermarket items in his coat and slipping out of the store. On one occasion a staff member followed, asking why he had left without paying. They clashed and Cook was charged with assault. The case was dismissed in court.

With his father still dabbling in speed, Jarryd looked after him as much as Cook looked after his teenage son.

'We got through on the bones of our arse,' Cook says. 'I said to him one day, "When the world goes up, there will be me and you and the cockroaches." No matter what happened, I knew we'd get by. And we did.'

Jarryd had wanted the family to stay together. But after seeing the years of arguing, he understood his mother's decision to go to Horsham and regain her independence. 'It was something she had to do,' he says. 'She'd never really done anything for herself.'

Despite the constant moving and his parents' drug use, he says he and his siblings had happy childhoods. There was always love in the house, toys to play with and food in the cupboard. 'Us kids always came first,' he says. 'I never went to school feeling sorry for myself or thinking it was bad at home. When I'd come home, mum would always ask me how my day was and dad would pretend that he cared, even if he didn't because of his state of mind.'

When he got older he realised his upbringing had been different to those of friends. Visiting their homes, he never saw bowls of marijuana on the kitchen bench.

Jarryd remembers the struggle to put food on the table and maintain roadworthy and registered cars when he and his father lived at the caravan park, and then in an emergency house at Rosebud. It was a tough time, but enjoyable in its own way. They often laughed at how bad things had become (Sally Desmond asserts that humour has been the one constant in her husband's life in the thirty years she's known him; without it he would have 'gone right over the edge').

Jarryd began to regard his father more as a mate than a figure of authority. It's held; they still talk four or five times a day. They still chuckle about the time Cook let Jarryd get behind the wheel of a Statesman he bought when he was sixteen or seventeen. They'd gone to a football match at Tyabb and on the way back Jarryd, wanting to impress his girlfriend, begged his father to let him drive. Cook said yes. Police began following the Statesman and pulled them over.

Cook panicked. Jarryd said, 'Dad, you've just had a heart attack.'

When the police tapped at the window of the car, Cook feigned pain and put his hands over his chest. An ambulance was called, and he was given morphine and taken to Rosebud Hospital. The doctors found nothing wrong with him and couldn't explain the episode. He was released later that night. The unlicensed teenager had pulled off a shifty that left his father marvelling at his quick thinking and ingenuity.

Jarryd, who left school at fifteen to become an apprentice vehicle body builder, had often driven while unlicensed to get to work. Once he was caught by police in a beat-up Ford Falcon wagon he was filling with petrol in South Gippsland. Police confiscated the key.

Jarryd phoned his father, asking what he should do. 'You've got a spare key, haven't you?' Cook asked. He confirmed he had. 'Well you better get in the car and get home because I need to get to work tomorrow.' So, with no plates on the unregistered car, the seventeen-year-old set out for Rosebud. As illegal as it was, he says, it had to be done to bring in money.

As for his father's drug-taking, he says: 'He put us first, but when he had a bit of spare money he'd have times where he'd go off. But it was never benders that lasted weeks. I'd heard about those. They weren't there anymore. It was more a dabble.'

It remained so when Cook got himself on the payroll at the Martha Cove Marina project. It was the best money he had earned since the Station Hotel, the days when money flowed through his hands like water. At last, he and Jarryd didn't have to wonder where their next meal was coming from.

Seeing signs announcing the marina development, he turned up to the site unannounced, saying he was looking for work and was 'reliable and honest, and I'll show up every day'.

Cook was given a job driving an earth-moving truck. He rolled it twice, suffering nothing more serious than a ribbing from colleagues. Jarryd teased him, too.

When he was younger, Jarryd never challenged his father about his drug use. How could a kid tell an adult what to do? But when he turned eighteen, he began to tell his father he needed to get himself clean. He always thought it would take a 'wake-up' call with his health for Cook to turn his back on drugs once and for all.

It came in 2008, when he had a mild angina attack. He went to the doctor, who called an ambulance. While being treated in hospital, Cook picked up an infection to the heart. It necessitated a three-month stay, a drip in his arm feeding him antibiotics every four hours.

Cook had turned sixty. Despite his years on amphetamines, he had always looked younger than his age. But the infection took a toll. 'He really came crashing down, started looking old,' Jarryd says. 'He was very sick. He was actually forgetting the names of people — Mum, Jordan, Jaimee, everyone. He'd ask me what had happened and where he was, and I'd tell him. Thirty seconds later, he'd ask me again.'

Cook says the heart infection 'knocked the shit out of me' and got him thinking about his health. Until then, he thought his body could handle anything. But, as Desmond had a few years earlier, he realised he couldn't go on living the way he was. He wanted to be around for his children, sharing their journeys into adulthood and parenthood.

A female doctor told him: 'Go back to your wicked ways and you will die, Mr Cook.' The words shook him.

His illness made the television news. 'A football icon is on the comeback after a serious health scare,' Channel 9 reported. 'VFA legend Fred Cook has had his share of highs and lows, but two months in hospital have changed his life for the better. Drug addiction led the great full forward in and out of court and jail, but this has given him a new take on life.'

Cook said he'd seen two men die in hospital and he wasn't ready to join them. He also said Jaimee, then twelve, didn't need the upset of arriving at hospital and being told her father was seriously ill.

After he recovered, Cook, by now living in the Ministry of Housing property in Mornington, worked on the Eastlink roads project. He enjoyed the money and the routine of getting out of bed every day. And he found he could cope without speed, even if there was always a 'little man' in his head reminding him of the high it could bring.

Cook says his separation from drugs was like losing a friend with whom he'd shared many great times. But there could be no more. 'That lady doctor got in my head,' he says. 'Christ, I had to start looking after myself or it was all over.'

In the next few years he made regular court appearances, mainly for driving offences. The media stopped reporting them; it was as if repetition had made them tedious, like a joke told too often.

When Cook next popped up in *The Herald Sun*, he was writing a full-page article about the fall of West Coast Eagles champion Ben Cousins. Cousins, he wrote, 'probably thinks he is bullet proof … It's like a magic ride at the Royal Melbourne Show. It's exhilarating. But he'll learn. What goes up must come down.'

He went on: 'It's fair to say that I should be dead now. It was more good luck than good fortune that I am still here today.'

ı|||ı

AFTER the death of Fred Cook senior in 2008, Cook received about $80,000 when the family house in Yarraville was sold. Family members told him to use it wisely and perhaps set some aside in a high-interest bank account.

But he tore through it, handing it out like Santa Claus, his friend Chris Martin says. 'He thought he was some kind of millionaire,' Martin recalls, relating how Cook gave a few thousand to an acquaintance whose wife had left him. 'He was dropping in to so many houses that I thought he was back on the gear. It was ridiculous. I couldn't believe it. He thought it was like the old days, when he had an endless amount of cash.'

Six months later, Martin says, he was picking Cook up and taking him out for dinner because there was no food in the house.

Cook gave some money to Sally Desmond and his children. Jarryd bought a large flat-screen television, Jordan a sound system and Jaimee a computer.

'I felt like I'd let the kids down at certain stages,' he says. 'So while I had it, I was happy to top them up. It was probably a way to clear my conscience.'

Cook, never car savvy but always liking good wheels under him, paid $12,000 for a 2004 two-door Mercedes-Benz Kompressor that had been written off. He figured that if he spent $5000 or $6000 having it repaired, he'd have a car worth $35,000. But it didn't turn out that way and it ended up costing him about $30,000. Jarryd was angry, believing his father had been ripped off. Cook let it go. 'Life's too short,' he told his son. Jarryd says, 'It was a shemozzle, but there was nothing we could do about it.'

He also donated money to the Salvation Army, his way of paying it back for the times it gave him Christmas hampers, food parcels and toys for his children when he was broke. Cook says the Salvos never let him down. 'They're a good mob. I sling them something when I can.'

Earning more than $2000 a week on the Peninsula road project, he also began sponsoring an overseas aid program for underprivileged children. When the link from Frankston to Mt Martha was finished and he was again scratching for work, he could no longer contribute to the program. It pained him to cease payments.

'Even when he had to go on the pension, he deliberated for about a month about whether he could give up on these poor kids,' Jarryd says. 'He's always been quite loose with his money. But when he has it he tries to put it in the right places.'

ı|lı

ALL the great names are there. It's a roll call of football's finest. Darrel Baldock, Ron Barassi, Kevin Bartlett, Haydn Bunton senior, Barry Cable, Roy Cazaly, John Coleman, Gordon Coventry, Jack Dyer, Graham Farmer, Royce Hart, Peter Hudson, Bill Hutchison, Alex Jesaulenko, Jock McHale, Kevin Murray, Leigh Matthews, John Nicholls, Bob Pratt, Dick Pratt, Barrie Robran, Bob Skilton, Norm Smith, Ian Stewart and Ted Whitten take their place as official legends in the Australian Football Hall of Fame. And underneath them are dozens of champion players, including Gary Ablett, Nathan Buckley, Wayne Carey, Bob Davis, Jason Dunstall, James Hird, Tony Lockett, Sam Newman, Michael Tuck, Michael Voss and Greg Williams.

In 2006, Football Victoria (now AFL Victoria) considered nominating Fred Cook to join such august company.

Although he hadn't played much league football, he had been a champion in a competition that for many years contested the national football carnival. And his accomplishments were many: 300 VFA games, 1336 goals, six premierships and a J. J. Liston Trophy.

But Football Victoria never nominated Cook or another champion association goalkicker, Ron Todd. It did, however, put up Port Melbourne's other great champion, Frank Johnson, who went to South Melbourne after winning five best and fairests and two All Australian jumpers at the Borough — and promptly won another in his first season as a Swan in 1960. Johnson was inducted into the Hall of Fame in 2007.

'At that stage, we were testing the water with regards to the Hall of Fame, and we thought we'd put up the VFA's most decorated player. We judged that player to be Frank Johnson,' former VFL general manager Martin Stillman recalls. 'I think the idea was to see if we could get one in, then try to get a few more in, guys like Fred Cook and maybe [Williamstown's] Gerry Callahan.'

Stillman left the league in 2008. Since then, no more VFA players have been nominated.

On the AFL website, the Australian Football Hall of Fame is said to 'recognise and enshrine players, coaches, umpires, administrators and media representatives who have made significant contributions to Australian football — at any level — since the game's inception in 1858'.

The committee assesses candidates on their record, ability, integrity, sportsmanship and character. In 2013, Adelaide football writer and Hall of Fame committee member Michelangelo Rucci put Cook up for consideration. League protocol prevents him from discussing it, but Sam Newman says he understands Rucci put much thought and research into the Port Melbourne great, and concluded he would be a worthy nominee.

Newman is adamant his old friend belongs in the Hall of Fame despite his off-field wrongdoings.

'Obviously, Fred fails one of the criteria for admission to the Hall of Fame — character,' he says. 'But here is the conundrum. The overwhelming mainstay of condition of entry is that one excels in the physical skills of Australian Rules football. You don't have to be a nuclear physicist, have a formal education, live on the right side of the river or live a conventional life. What you do have to have is the capacity to take your life back after adversity has paid you a visit. The Hall of Fame is scattered with inductees who have erred. But to be sent to purgatory forever is un-Australian, even unchristian. Someday, Fred should be inducted. It will be an interesting acceptance speech at least!'

Until a few years ago, Cook was unaware the Hall of Fame existed (it was established in 1996). But he's gone through the list of inducted players and says it would be an honour to join them.

He has no opinion on whether he should be in it, believing it's up to others to judge his achievements. He understands his off-field issues will give him no easy passage. 'If it happens, it happens. I'm not going to lose any sleep over it,' Cook says. 'But just in case they're thinking about it, I'd better not import any drugs in from Colombia.'

More certain was Cook's recognition from Port Melbourne in May 2014, when it announced it would be naming an end behind the goals at North Port Oval after him. The other end would honour Bob Bonnett, the club's other great goalkicker. An unveiling was planned for June. Cook's first reaction was that the Borough should be naming a bay of the Norm Goss Grandstand after him, so many goals did he kick in it with female company after dark.

When a local paper phoned him for comment, he preferred to speak about Bonnett, who he admired as a player and a clubman. 'He kicks more than 900 goals in the seniors, and then he's happy to drop back and captain-coach the seconds and help the kids. That's the mark of the man.'

When he was playing, Cook would often see Bonnett's wife, June, in the social rooms and shout, 'Hey, Junie, who's the second best full forward in the history of Port Melbourne?' 'You are, Fred,' she would reply with a laugh.

The Port Melbourne announcement was a pick-me-up for Cook. Chris Martin had been struck down with a brain tumour, and fellow J. J. Liston Trophy winner Derek King died of cancer after it invaded his bowel and liver. King was sixty-five.

Cook met Martin, forty-five, on the construction of the marina, and they were also colleagues on the Eastlink and Peninsula Link road projects. He credits Martin with keeping him in work after Desmond left and he badly needed it. They catch up once a week and regularly talk on the phone. 'Can't believe it,' Cook said when told Martin had collapsed in the Melbourne city centre. 'Two weeks ago he was as fit as a fiddle. Now, Jesus, he's got a battle in front of him.'

King and Cook played together in VFA teams, and Cook held the speedy rover in high regard, as a footballer and fellow. He was taken aback by King's death. 'Too young,' he says. 'Christ, he was younger than me.' Through an intermediary, he sent his condolences to the family.

Three weeks after King's passing, Preston champion Laurie Hill also succumbed to illness. Hill won the J. J. Liston Trophy twice, either side of Cook's victory in 1970. It was another reminder of his own mortality.

The court case was also playing on his mind. He was relieved when it was adjourned in March, giving Bernie Balmer eight weeks to work on that miracle. Cook had to present to Frankston for a pre-sentence report and Clifton Hill for a psychiatric evaluation. The trip to Clifton Hill was an ordeal; he had to battle bumper-to-bumper traffic on the Monash Freeway. 'How long's this been going on? Christ, I could have walked and got there quicker,' he said.

Highlighting the long list of prior convictions, Balmer had confided before the court case that Cook was staring at his fourth jail sentence.

18

FRED Cook last appeared in court on drug charges in 1998, relating to the marijuana plants in the Safety Beach shed that he would light up like a Christmas tree in the middle of the night. But most years since, he's had to call on Bernie Balmer for his legal expertise.

Cars and Cook go together about as well as moccasins and puddles. He is competent behind the wheel, but when police have pulled him over they've often had to reach for the charge sheet, for offences ranging from driving while to disqualified to ignoring traffic signs to talking on his mobile phone. As a result, Balmer is on good terms with the Road Safety Act.

As he says, it's as if Cook has a flashing red light on the roof of his car to alert police that he is on the road.

In the past twelve years, Cook has fronted these courts:

- Frankston on 8 August 2002, for driving while disqualified and over the speed limit. He received a $400 fine.
- Frankston on 3 August 2007, again for driving while disqualified, driving while his licence was suspended, failing to wear a seatbelt and using a hand-held telephone. Cook was jailed for one month, with the sentence to be served as an intensive correction order.

- Dandenong on 2 November 2007, for failing to obey a no-stopping sign. Cook was fined $115.
- Frankston on 4 September 2009, for two counts of driving while his licence was suspended, failing to diverge left and using a mobile phone. The magistrate jailed him for two months, suspending the sentence for twelve months.
- Frankston on 19 April 2010, for two counts of driving while his licence was suspended, owning an unregistered vehicle and exceeding a 100 kilometre per hour speed limit. Jailed for thirty days, Cook appealed in the Melbourne County Court, but abandoned it and did his time at the Melbourne Remand Centre.
- Dromana on 28 February 2013, for driving while his licence was suspended and failing to wear a 'properly adjusted or fastened' seatbelt. He received a four-month prison term, suspended for two years, and was disqualified from driving for two months.

Cook did the wheeling and his lawyer did the legal dealing. But it had to stop, Balmer said after the February 2013 hearing. There could be no more charges. He told Cook he had been lucky to get another suspended sentence, but it couldn't keep happening. 'It won't,' Cook replied.

A fortnight later, Balmer got a phone call from Cook. Police had pinched him again in what the lawyer calls 'almost comical circumstances'.

After the hearing, he had left his car at Dromana because it wouldn't turn over. It sat there for a week, prompting complaints to the local council. Cook couldn't afford to have it towed. Lugging a battery, he caught a bus from Mornington to Dromana, got the vehicle started and set out for home. But he was intercepted on the Nepean Highway, and was charged with driving while disqualified and using an unregistered car.

Balmer says, 'I said to him, "Why couldn't you have thought it through for a change?" Why not get someone else to take it home? He just didn't think. He never does. So here we are again. I get frustrated because there is a ripple affect, on his kids, on Sally. They don't want to see him keep going up [to court].'

On the eve of the 28 May hearing, Cook owned up to being apprehensive. In the previous days he had been phoning Balmer and saying, 'Well, how are you going to get me out of this?'

He had been to jail and he knew he wasn't facing a hanging offence, but he was tired of going to court and sweating about the outcome. It played on his nerves. It wasn't good for his health. 'I'm too old for this shit,' he was saying. He spoke about staging a heart attack in court if things weren't going his way.

The following day, he arrived at Frankston Magistrates' Court at 9.50am. The case was to be heard in the small sixth court. He met Balmer outside it. 'Couldn't have combed your hair for the occasion, Fred?' Balmer asked. He mumbled something about running late.

Cook took a seat at the back of the court. He was restless, picking at a scab on his right arm, scratching his hair, rubbing his hands together, fidgeting with the mobile phone in the pocket of his white shirt and squeezing his packet of Bond Street Red cigarettes.

Others cases took up the next ninety minutes — a young man charged with assaulting his girlfriend, a chronic cannabis user being assessed for rehabilitation, a motor mechanic up for speeding while already on a suspended sentence for driving while disqualified.

Cook slipped out for a cigarette and resumed his seat five minutes later. 'Why don't they have ashtrays in the toilet anymore?' he asked. At one point, he commented loudly on a case, prompting Balmer to spin around and give him a look of admonishment.

Cook's court name, Frederick Williams, was called at 11.40am. He rose from his seat and walked a few paces to sit behind his lawyer.

Magistrate Anne Goldsbrough read a pre-sentence report by Community Correctional Services in Frankston, and a psychiatric assessment prepared by Forensicare.

When she finished, Balmer said the purpose of the material was to highlight the 'exceptional circumstances' needed to convince the court to keep the suspended sentence in place. He said Cook was 'clearly a man absolutely fried by drug abuse' and had 'burned' his marriages and relationships with his children. 'We have a fellow with a lot of issues,' Balmer said.

Cook told the magistrate: 'I'm not a bad bloke, Your Honour. These days I use my powers for good, not evil.'

'That was not always the case, was it?' Goldsbrough replied.

She surprised Cook by saying that many years ago she had worked as an articled clerk in the office of his former Port Melbourne teammate Brendan Behan. As such, she had heard 'some of the stories' about him and other footballers who sought Behan's legal advice. 'That previous life has come through in these reports,' she said, noting a 'significant criminal history'.

Cook replied that he had lost about $5.3 million over the years and 'now all I've got is the $10 note in my back pocket'. He said he had volunteered to work two days a week with St Vincent de Paul in Mornington.

Police prosecutor Senior Constable Ross Treverton submitted

that Cook had 'mental health issues requiring some degree of mercy from the court'.

Goldsbrough described the circumstances of Cook's arrest as 'rather bizarre and somewhat ironic', but she said the psychiatric report 'helps me understand why your decision-making is flawed'.

She told Cook years of substance abuse had 'changed the way your brain works'. 'The decision to drive home was plain silly,' she said.

Then came her decision. Goldsbrough said it would be 'unduly harsh' to apply the suspended sentence considering his health problems. She imposed a two-month jail sentence for driving while disqualified, but suspended it for twelve months, and fined Cook $400 for having an unregistered vehicle, giving him two months to pay.

Relief washed over him. As with the adjournment hearing two months earlier, Cook left Goldsbrough with a quip: 'You should get a proper job, Your Honour, because you have great people skills.'

'Maybe in my next life,' she replied.

A few minutes later, a smiling Cook went outside for a cigarette. His phone rang. It was his son Jarryd. 'Yeah, mate, we've had a victory, got the result we were after,' he said, likening it to Port Melbourne coming from behind in the 1980 grand final against Coburg.

Balmer had another case straight after Cook's, but thirty minutes later they met at a café in the Bayside shopping centre across from the court house.

'All your stars aligned today,' Balmer said as Cook tipped five sugars into a large cappuccino. 'Had I been the judge I probably would have locked you up because you've had a lot of chances, Fred. This is your twelfth offence for driving while disqualified.'

Cook: 'Only the twelfth?'

Balmer: 'As I said, all your stars aligned, right through from the judge having known you when she was a solicitor starting out, looking after wayward Port Melbourne players.'

Cook: 'I was going to make a comment on that, but I thought I'd quit while I was ahead.'

Balmer: 'That's why I was standing there saying don't get ahead of yourself, just shut up. But I sincerely hope you learn from this. We must live within the law of the land, otherwise you have anarchy. You've got a very, very cavalier approach to the law, and the law has been very kind to you. With your experiences, you have a lot to offer and it's not much to repay the community for all the money and time that's been pumped into you. You owe 'em.'

Cook: 'Yeah. Suppose so. I'm going to chip in with Vinnies [St Vincent de Paul]. I saw two old blokes, Stan and Errol, coming down the street dropping off food and I said, "Any chance of jumping on the bandwagon?" I'm sick of watching Judge Judy.'

Balmer: 'You've just got to look in the mirror and understand the devastation you've extracted on yourself. You've been very unfair to yourself, you've been very unfair to your families, you've been very unfair to the community. Go and give a bit back. That will be a very good thing to do, Fred.'

Cook: 'Yeah, I accept that.'

Balmer: 'And stay out of trouble.'

Cook: 'I will. I promise.'

Balmer: 'I've heard that before, Fred.'

Acknowledgements

I saw Marc Fiddian's byline often during research for this book, in the online *Age* archive and on the covers of *The Pioneers: 100 Years of Association Football*; *The VFA: A History of the Victorian Football Association*; and *The Roar of the Crowd: A History of VFA Grand Finals*.

Marc Fiddian dedicated much of his skill to chronicling the VFA, and his books — the three mentioned above and his string of informative and entertaining club histories — must be the first point of reference for anyone wanting to gain an understanding and appreciation of the competition. It was a pleasure to read his accounts of matches and the players who shaped them.

Terry Keenan's excellent Port Melbourne Football Club history, *A Different Breed* (Volume 3), was always within arm's length, and Ken Linnett's *Game for Anything*, his splendid biography of Tom Lahiff, gave a fascinating insight into two admirable Borough men, Lahiff and Norm Goss.

Articles from *The Sporting Globe*, *Sun*, *Herald*, *Herald Sun*, *Age*, *Sunday Press*, *Inside Football* and the western suburbs community newspapers that covered Fred Cook were also invaluable.

There were interviews with Fred Cook, Ricky Spargo, Pam Cook, Gary Brice, Bernie Balmer, Gary Dempsey, John Schultz,

Laurie Sandilands, John Heriot, Alan Bongetti, Charlie Chrimes, Phil Cleary, Alan Wickes, Norm Brown, Bob Profitt, Graeme Anderson, Vic 'Stretch' Aanensen, David 'Sam' Holt, Billy Swan, Greg 'Biff' Dermott, Norm Goss junior, Peter Saultry, Bob Bonnett, Graham 'Buster' Harland, Stephen Phillips, Scot Palmer, Ian Collins, Harold Martin, Pat Flaherty, Allan Harper, Nigel Murch, Ron Joseph, Ross Glendinning, Mick Erwin, Phil Gibbs, Michael Lovett, Brendan Behan, Peter McKenna, Sam Newman, Kerry Foley, Geoff Poulter, Jan Smith, Doug Hawkins, Colin Kinnear, Tony Ebeyer, Sally Desmond, Steve Allender, Jason Love, Neville Stibbard, Martin Stillman, Ken Gannon, Karen McNamara, Kim McNamara, Barry Rowlings, Steve Barnes, Graham Stewart, Frank Vergona, Gordon Bennett, Charlie Bezzina, Kelvin Greenhill, Leo Cook, Barry Evans, David Glennie, Professor Jayashri Kulkarni, Bob Skilton, Ted Whitten junior, Brian Levier, Chris Martin, Jarryd Cook, Andrew Fraser, Joe Radojevic and Bob Doughty.

There was help from Peter Vesty, George Paras, Russell Holmesby, Barry Kidd, Gerry Walsh, Darren Arthur, John Heron, Natalie Kealey and Tony Cannatelli.

There was wise counsel from Andrew Rule, Paul Kennedy, Phil Cleary, Scot Palmer, Bruce Eva and Sam Newman. There was guidance from David Tenenbaum and the kindly and patient staff of Melbourne Books, which expressed interest in the book within 30 minutes of receiving a few chapters.

And there was support and encouragement from my wife, Nicole. Bless her.

The Author

Paul Amy is a sports journalist at *Leader Newspapers* and *Inside Football.* He spent most of his childhood in Fish Creek, South Gippsland, where his neighbour and former Richmond player John Ryan regaled him with tales about Captain Blood, Jack Dyer. He first watched football in the outer at Victoria Park, Collingwood, with his father, Bill, and can still remember the sight of big Len Thompson breasting the banner. He was also an avid viewer of VFA matches telecast on Channel 0. Paul is married with three daughters.

Fred Cook in the Square

The game was big
The crowds were there
Full backs were tough
Fred Cook was in the square

The VFA was played on Sundays
But people didn't care
Supporters thought it fun days
When Cook stood in the square

You either loved or loathed him
He'd always play but fair
A backline would surely sink than swim
When Cooky ruled the square

Many a player tried the bash
And Freddy copped his share
He always kicked a bagful
Our Freddy in the square

The opposition looked slow and short
Cooky played with flair
The 70s and 80s were great for Port
'Cause Number 5 owned the square

He played in six grand finals
The pressure? He didn't care
While others shook in their boots
Fred simply roamed the square

He won a Liston Trophy
He was captain of the Vics
He was captain of the Borough
And got his share of kicks

He has become a legend
With the media always there
He surely was heaven sent
OUR COOKY IN THE SQUARE

— Tony Cannatelli

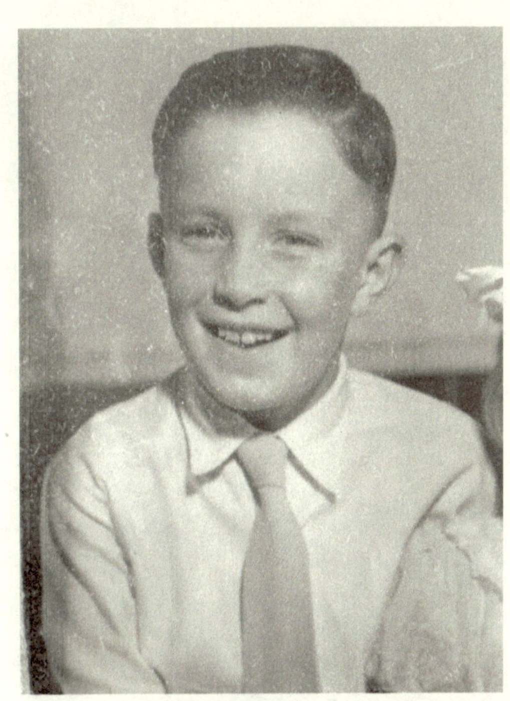

TOP Fred Cook at age nine. Courtesy of Pam Cook

BOTTOM The photo Cook would sign for his young fans. Courtesy of Fred Cook

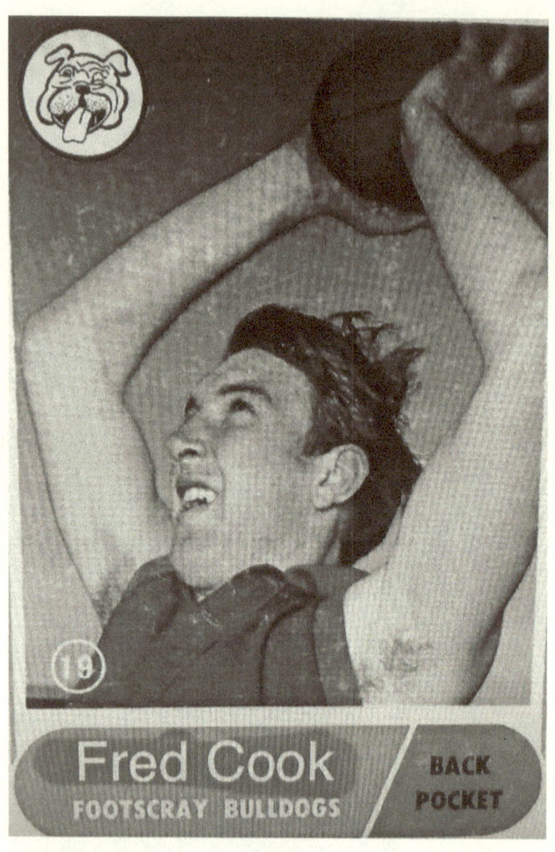

TOP Fred Cook's 1969 Scanlens football card. He was mistakenly named on the card as Ron McGowan. Courtesy of Gerry Walsh

BOTTOM Footscray Technical School old boys. Left to right: Noel Fincher, Fred Cook, Rod O'Connor and Gary Dempsey.

TOP Ted Whitten leads his players in a sprint at a midnight training session in 1969. Left to right: Ian Bryant, Ivan Marsh, Whitten, Fred Cook, John Jillard. Courtesy of Fred Cook

MIDDLE *The Sporting Globe's* football team in 1978. Left to right: Sam Newman, Fred Cook, Greg Hobbs and Adrian Gallagher. Courtesy of Fred Cook

BOTTOM Left to right: Bob Skilton, Fred Cook and Peter Bedford surround a birthday cake for 100 years of the VFA. Courtesy of Fred Cook

TOP Fred Cook senior and Fred Cook. Courtesy of Fred Cook

BOTTOM Fred Cook playing in front against Sandringham in 1977. Courtesy of Tony Cannatelli

Fred Cook as winner of Yarraville's J. J. Liston Trophy in 1970. Courtesy of Fred Cook

TOP Fred Cook plucks a mark in a match in 1976. Courtesy of Tony Cannatelli

BOTTOM The cover of the 1978 Victorian Football Association grand final. Courtesy of Fred Cook

TOP Fred Cook with actress Pat McDonald. Courtesy of Fred Cook

BOTTOM Fred Cook in a Port Melbourne legends match. Courtesy of Tony Cannatelli

Fred Cook front and almost centre in a VFA poster from the 1970s. Courtesy of Fred Cook

TOP Fred Cook and Mornington Peninsula Nepean Football League coach Barry Burke, father of St Kilda champion Nathan. Courtesy of Fred Cook

MIDDLE Fred Cook, Jack Klugman and Sam Newman at Moonee Valley Racecourse in the early 1980s. Courtesy of Sam Newman

BOTTOM Lil Goss, Norm Goss and Fred Cook. Courtesy of Lil Goss

TOP Marriage to Sally Desmond in 1999. Courtesy of Fred Cook

BOTTOM Sam Newman speaking as best man at the wedding of Fred Cook and Karen McNamara in 1985. Courtesy of Kim McNamara

TOP Fred Cook and Karen McNamara on their wedding day in 1985. Courtesy of Kim McNamara

BOTTOM The wedding party in 1985. Courtesy of Kim McNamara

Fred Cook behind the bar of his Station Hotel. Courtesy of Kim McNamara

TOP Fred Cook senior,
Fred Cook and son Jarryd.
Courtesy of Fred Cook

BOTTOM Fred Cook and Sally
Desmond with baby Jarryd.
Courtesy of Fred Cook

Fred Cook and family at North Port Oval in June 2014. Left to right: Ricky Kline, Jaimee Cook, Sally Desmond, Trey Campbell, Fred Cook, Briana Cook, Jess Malm, Jarryd Cook and Jordan Cook. Courtesy of Sally Desmond

Fred Cook and Phil Cleary take a ride around Etihad Stadium before the 2008 VFL grand final. Radio SEN's Mark Stone puts a question to Cook.
Courtesy of Tony Cannatelli

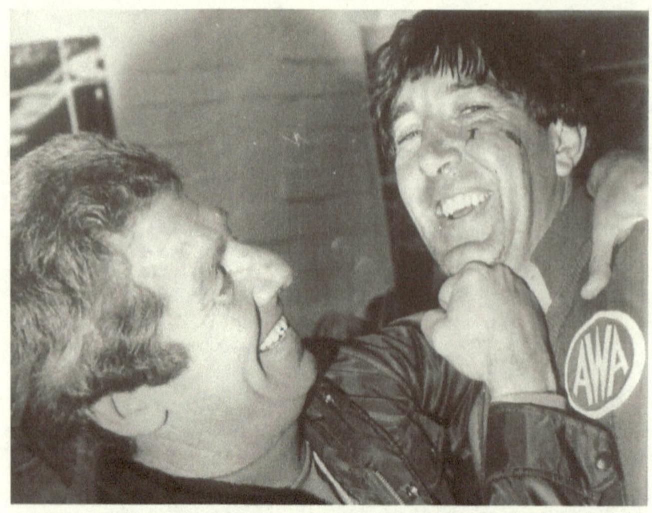

TOP Bob Bonnett playfully pops Fred Cook on the chin after Cook passed his VFA goalkicking record. Courtesy of Bob Bonnett

BOTTOM Port Melbourne greats Fred Cook and Bob Bonnett at North Port Oval in June 2014. Courtesy of Fred Cook

www.ingramcontent.com/pod-product-compliance
Lightning Source LLC
LaVergne TN
LVHW050952080826
845145LV00005B/1480

* 9 7 8 1 9 2 2 1 2 9 4 7 5 *